Englisch lernen mit Berlitz®

Kate Atkinson

Waste of Love

Berlitz Publishing
München • New York • Singapur

Berlitz Englisch lernen mit Kate Atkinson
Waste of Love

Vokabelerklärungen und Übungen: Berit Lina Barth
Lektorat: Anna Egger
Layout: Ute Weber
Cover-Gestaltung: Svea Stoss
Projektleitung: Eva Betz

Berlitz Publishing
Mies-van-der-Rohe-Straße 1
D-80807 München

Satz: Franzis print & media GmbH, München
Druck: Mercedes-Druck, Berlin
Printed in Germany
ISBN 978-3-468-79245-8

10010

Inhalt

Liebe Leserin, lieber Leser,

mit den unterhaltsamen Kurzgeschichten von Kate Atkinson halten Sie endlich ein Englischbuch in der Hand, das Sie garantiert nicht mehr weglegen wollen. Und vor lauter Witz und Spannung merken Sie vielleicht gar nicht, dass Sie ganz nebenbei auch Ihre Englischkenntnisse gehörig auffrischen und erweitern.
Damit Ihr Lesevergnügen nicht durch das Nachschlagen unbekannter Wörter gemindert wird, sind die schwierigsten Vokabeln im Text blau markiert und in der Marginalspalte übersetzt. Interessante Wörter, die in einer Infobox erklärt werden, sind zusätzlich mit einem Sternchen gekennzeichnet. Alle übersetzten Wörter sind außerdem im Wörterverzeichnis im Anhang zusammengefasst.
Allein beim Schmökern in den Kurzgeschichten können Sie sehr viel dazulernen. Vielleicht möchten Sie aber auch Ihr Grammatikwissen und Ihre Vokabelkenntnisse zusätzlich erweitern oder aber Ihr Textverständnis prüfen. Zu diesem Zweck finden Sie auf jeder Doppelseite knifflige und unterhaltsame Übungen. Die Vokabeln aus dem Text werden dort noch einmal verwendet und bleiben dadurch viel besser im Gedächtnis haften – so können Sie später leichter darauf zurückgreifen. Selbstverständlich sind auch die Lösungen zu allen Übungen im Anhang abgedruckt.

Und nun wünschen wir Ihnen viel Spaß beim Lesen!
Ihre Berlitz-Redaktion

Joy and Woe are woven fine,
A Clothing for the Soul divine
Under every grief and pine
Runs a joy with wilken twine.

WILLIAM BLAKE, *AUGURIES OF INNOCENCE*

Tunnel of Fish

If Eddie could have chosen, he would have been a fish. A large fish without enemies, free to spend all day swimming lazily amongst the reeds and rushes in clear, blood-cold water. His mother, June, said not to worry, he was halfway there already, with his mouth hanging open all the time like a particularly dull-witted amphibian, not to mention the thick lenses of his spectacles that made his eyes bulge like a haddock's. Afterwards, of course, June had regretted saying that, but sometimes Eddie was so infuriatingly gormless that she couldn't help herself. June had hoped that the removal of his adenoids when he was eight would make Eddie look more intelligent. It hadn't. She had had the same expectations at nine for his spectacles. Most people she knew looked brainier with glasses, yet somehow Eddie contrived to look even more dopey. June thought that the grommets in his ears at ten would raise him from the undersea world of the deaf, and theoretically they had done, according to his ENT consultant, yet Eddie still behaved as if he couldn't hear a word June said. Which was just as well, June thought, seeing as half the time the things she said to him were not very nice.

For reasons best known to himself, Eddie had recently become an obsessive cataloguer of fish. He had already worked his way through shells, coins, stamps and flags. June wondered, not for the first time, if Eddie was mildly autistic. She hoped his eccentricities were genetic and nothing to do with her haphazard mothering.

It was a year now since Eddie had started secondary school and every day June expected a policeman at the

Feinde • Schilf • Binsen • kalt

einfältig • Brille • ließen … hervortreten • Schellfisch • zum Verzweifeln • dämlich • Rachenmandeln

gelang es, noch dämlicher auszusehen • Paukenröhrchen • (= ear, nose and throat) HNO-Arzt

besessen • Katalogisierer • Muscheln • Eigenartigkeiten • planlos

weiterführende Schule

door, telling her that her son had been beaten to a pulp in a corner of the playground or thrown himself in boyish despair from the top of the science block. (June was a pessimist by nature.) Eddie, June knew, was exactly the sort of boy whom even kind children were exasperated into bullying and normally decent teachers were driven to persecute. In some ways it was a relief when, at the school's first parents' evening, June discovered that none of Eddie's teachers had any idea who he was.

June was carrying Hawk's child. She liked that phrase, 'carrying a child'. 'Pregnant' made her think of animals – cows and sows and dogs, and the hamster ('Hammy') which was the only pet her parents would let her have when she was a child because both of them were ridden with allergies. She had felt sorry for Hammy's solitary existence, mirroring her own, and had let him play with her friend's hamster, Jock, and 'play' turned out to be a euphemism and 'him' turned out to be a 'her' and the outcome was that June ended up with a litter of tiny naked rodents that looked like miniature piglets and which gave her the creeps. 'Oh, June,' her mother sighed when she saw them. That

zu Brei geschlagen • Pausenhof • Verzweiflung • naturwissenschaftlicher Trakt • nett • waren so entnervt, dass sie … schikanierten • anständig • zu verfolgen • Elternabend • Redensart • ein Kind austragen • Säue • Haustier • waren von Allergien geplagt • einsam • Ergebnis • Wurf • Nager • Ferkel • ihr nicht geheuer waren

Übung 1 Welche phrases (Redewendungen) gehören zusammen? Verbinden Sie die beiden Teile mit einer Linie.

to be beaten	dead
to carry	allergies
to give somebody	to a pulp
to drop	having a standard life
to be ridden with	one's pathetic fears
to come across	the creeps
to shrug off	too many accidents
to be terrified of	a child

was what she always said – 'Oh, June' – so much disappointment packed into two such small words.
June didn't inherit her parents' allergies although that didn't stop them from expecting her to drop dead at any moment, if not of an out-of-the-blue asthma attack then from choking on a sweet or being run over by a car (or a bike or a train, not to mention being decapitated by a low-flying plane, as if such things were common in Edinburgh). Her father was a risk assessor for Standard Life and said that he came across too many accidents, bizarre or otherwise, to ignore the danger that lurked around every corner. The worst thing was that having spent her childhood and adolescence shrugging off their pathetic fears she was completely prey to them herself now.
June blamed her parents. June blamed her parents for everything, although it seemed a bit of a shame to blame her father, who had died in his bed, not from an accident but 'worn out' according to June's mother. 'By what?' June asked. 'By his life,' her mother said. His standard life. That was the one thing that June had been terrified of having – a standard life, an ordinary life, a life like her parents' – living in a pink sandstone semi-detached villa in the suburbs with a neat

hatte … nicht geerbt • tot umzufallen • aus heiterem Himmel • zu ersticken • geköpft • Risikoprüfer • er sei auf … gestoßen • lauerten • Jugendzeit • abzutun • erbärmlich • wurde sie … von ihnen befallen • gab … die Schuld • verbraucht • vor der June große Angst gehabt hatte • Doppelhaushälfte • Stadtrand • hübsch

Übung 2

Sind die folgenden Aussagen richtig oder falsch? Tragen Sie ein T für true oder ein F für false in die Kästchen ein.

1. June wasn't allowed to have pets when she was a child.
2. June had two hamsters, a male and a female one.
3. June's parents always feared something awful might happen to their daughter.
4. According to June's mother her husband died of choking on a sweet.
5. June didn't want to lead an ordinary life.
6. A semi-detached villa in the suburbs was June's dream.

garden and an en-suite master bedroom with fitted wardrobes. Now she would rather like it. In their flat they didn't even have a bath, just a shower and a toilet. And a wardrobe, fitted or otherwise, would have been a great improvement on the overloaded garment rail on which they all kept their clothes.

großes Schlafzimmer mit eigenem Bad • Einbauschränke • Verbesserung • überladen • Kleiderstange

And also June could see that once you were thirty – which she was three weeks ago – it was probably time to stop holding your parents responsible for all the things that had gone wrong in your life, especially as if she had taken their advice she would now have a degree and a job and a decent house and probably even a husband instead of living in a crappy tenement with Eddie and Hawk, and Hawk only living with them anyway because he didn't have anywhere else to live.

(Hochschul-)Abschluss • nett • Scheiß- • Mietshaus

There was the dog as well, which didn't help. Tammy was an overenthusiastic terrier-cross that she'd got from the dogs' home at Seafield so that Eddie wouldn't have to spend his childhood without a pet the way she had, but then of course it turned out that the allergies had only skipped a generation and Eddie snuffled and sneezed and wheezed every time the dog got near him, which was all the time because the flat was so small. And the dog was pregnant. Carrying puppies.

überfreundlich • Terriermischling • Tierheim • hatten … übersprungen • schniefte • nieste • keuchte • Welpen

Übung 3

In jeder Zeile steht ein Wort, das nicht zu den anderen passt. Streichen Sie es durch.

1. old-fashioned – modern – ancient – former

2. snuffle – sneeze – shuffle – wheeze

3. decent – nice – neat – crappy

4. news – sitcom – soap opera – comedy

5. bath – bedroom – en-suite – kitchen

June was just eighteen when she had Eddie (what a big, sorrowful 'Oh, June' that was) whereas her mother was forty-two when she had June. June fully expected to be dead by the time she was forty-two. Her parents were old, really old. That was why they'd given her such an old-fashioned name. June, because she was born in June. If she'd been born in November would they have called her November? June was a name for women in sitcoms and soap operas, the name of women who knit with synthetic wool and follow recipes that use cornflakes, not the name of a thirty-year-old with a ring in her nose ('Oh, June').
At least she knew she was pregnant this time – for the first five months of Eddie's unfledged existence she had just thought she was getting disgustingly fat. Of course, June had never really wanted Eddie and in her heart she was sure that had she wanted him he would have turned out a different child – a loud, rude, shouting boy who ran around football pitches and had no fear and no defects. June knew that Hawk's baby was her second chance, the only way she could redeem herself for the mess she had made the first time round.

Eddie wanted to scramble back down the evolutionary ladder. He wanted gills instead of a clogged-up nose. And scales of silver and pearl instead of his own pale-and-prone-to-dermatitis skin. Eddie wondered if there was such a word as 'unevolving'. He had a list of Latin prefixes in the ancient Latin grammar that Hawk had found in a skip and he had been trying to teach himself the language ever since. Eddie didn't go to the kind of school where Latin had ever featured on the curriculum. There was a mystical power to Latin names. When he incanted the gorgeously impenetrable names of fish – *Pomacanthus imperator* (the Emperor Angelfish), *Zandus cornutus* (the Moorish Idol!) – Eddie felt like a sorcerer.

sorgenvoll

altmodisch

Sitcoms (= Situationskomödien) • Seifenopern • unreif • widerlich • unverschämt • Fußballplätze • mit dem sie sich von dem Durcheinander freimachen konnte • hinunterklettern • Kiemen • verstopft • Schuppen • blass und zu entzündlichen Reaktionen neigend • sich nicht entwickelnd • Vorsilben • uralt • Müllcontainer • auf dem Lehrplan gestanden hatte • aufsagte • hinreißend • unergründlich • Zauberer

In-volve, re-volve, de-volve. Eddie pored over the grammar and stroked an imaginary beard. '"Retro-volve", perhaps, professor,' he said out loud to himself in a silly voice. Most of Eddie's conversations were with himself. His mother thought he was being bullied at school but Eddie knew he wasn't important enough in the school hierarchy to be bullied. He was part of the ranks of the invisible, but it was OK, there were quite a lot of invisible boys, they formed an unofficial, invisible club. They made feeble jokes to themselves about themselves – the Ancient Geeks, Geek Gods – and they all secretly believed that the geeks would inherit the earth.

A few months ago, Hawk had found an old fish tank and a goldfish to put in it but the fish had never thrived and had acquired all kinds of strange lumps and fungal growths until it was a relief when it went bleached and belly-up and put Eddie out of his misery. That was pretty much when Eddie had lost faith in Hawk. He knew how to get things but he didn't how to keep them.

Hawk's real name was 'Alan' which didn't have the same heroic ring to it. Hawk was English, from Cheshire, a place that was a mystery to both June and Eddie, who could think only of cheese and cats. His raptorial soubriquet was the result of a night in a sweat lodge in the Highlands when his true self – the hawk-headed sun god Ra – was revealed to him. 'Kind of like a totem,' he explained to Eddie. Eddie didn't tell Hawk that he also knew his own true identity – revealed to him by a huge, solid carp, patterned like blue and white marble, that lived in a pond in the hot-houses in the Botanics. Eddie knew it was his totem because it had spoken to him.

Eddie often thought about the baby inside June. He had been charting its embryonic progress with an old medical encyclopaedia from the same skip haul as his Latin grammar. From tiny tadpole to gilled fish to

brütete über • streichelte • gedacht • Bart

die Reihen der Unsichtbaren • lahm • (statt: Ancient Greeks; Greek Gods) • Streber • Aquarium • war nicht gediehen • Geschwülste • Pilzbefall • ausgebleicht • mit dem Bauch nach oben • nicht so heldenhaft klang • (County im westl. Mittelengland) • räuberisch • Spitzname • schottisches Hochland • mit einem Falkenkopf • Re (ägypt. Sonnengott) • Karpfen • (= Botanical Gardens) botanischer Garten • erfasst • Beute • Kaulquappe

froggy foetus, he had wondered about his unborn sibling. Brother or sister, he hadn't really minded, he just thought that it would be nice to have someone else in his family. Now it seemed it was going to be a girl, which Eddie thought would probably be better for his mother. He kept the ultrasound photograph of his soon-to-be sister by the side of his bed.

Bruder oder Schwester • war ihm egal gewesen

Ultraschallbild • zukünftig

June rubbed baby oil onto her stomach. The skin on her belly was like a drum. The drum was being beaten from the inside in an irregular tom-tom and she wondered if the baby was kicking or punching. The baby was a girl. The technician doing the ultrasound had asked her did she want to know the sex or did she want to be surprised. June hated surprises. She had been surprised enough when she found out she was pregnant with Eddie. She wasn't surprised this time because she had stopped taking the pill and she pretty much only had to look at a man and, hey presto, she was pregnant. Carrying.
Sometimes June wondered if she attracted fertility. In the olden days she would probably have been burned as a sacrifice or something to help the crops.
Eddie wasn't her first. There was the sexless embryo

Tamtam

Simsalabim

Fruchtbarkeit • früher • Opfer (-gabe) • Ernte

Einige Wörter sind nicht vollständig. Ergänzen Sie die fehlenden Buchstaben.

Übung 4

1. Eddie liked to look at the __ __ t __ __ s __ __ n __ photograph of the sister he soon would have.
2. Sometimes you have to give something away as a __ a __ __ i __ i __ __.
3. Eddie studied the grammar and __ t __ __ k __ __ a beard that wasn't there.
4. In the __ __ t __ n __ __ s you can see plants and some animals like fish and birds.
5. A frog starts out as a tiny __ __ d p __ __ __.

hatte beseitigt werden müssen • wollte davon nichts wissen

that had had to be disposed of when she was fifteen ('Oh, June'). Her mother had tried to persuade her to keep it but June was having none of it. Now she thought about it a lot. A 'foetus', she'd taught herself to say over the years, but now it had become a baby again in her mind. Not that she was against abortions in any way. Terminated. It always made her think of Arnold Schwarzenegger*. She was the terminator*. It would have been fourteen and it wouldn't be an it, it would be a boy or a girl, an older brother or sister for Eddie, someone to guide him and be a friend (and, God knows, he could do with one). Maybe that was why she was having this baby. To make up. To atone. Hawk was very surprised by her pregnancy, of course, because he didn't know about her coming off the pill and she told him it must have stopped working because she was sick that one time. She hoped the baby would make Hawk stay. Clip his wings. Although she knew it wouldn't.

Abtreibungen • Beendet.

Zur Wiedergutmachung. • Um zu büßen.

Seine Flügel stutzen.

She was glad it was a girl because she hadn't had much success with a boy. She could buy pretty clothes for a girl and plait her hair with ribbons. And she could call her a nice, old-fashioned, middle-class name like Sarah or Emma or Hannah. A girl would like dolls and

flechten • Bänder

info

Arnold Schwarzenegger ist seit 2003 Gouverneur von Kalifornien. Der 1947 geborene Österreicher wanderte 1968 in die USA aus, wo er sich als Immobilienmakler ein Vermögen aufbaute. Auch im Sport war er sehr erfolgreich – der Bodybuilder wurde mehrfach „Mr. Universum". Als Schauspieler wurde er vor allem durch die „Terminator"-Filme bekannt. Der erste dieser mittlerweile vier Science-Fiction-Filme stammt aus dem Jahr 1984. Schwarzenegger spielt darin einen „Cyborg", dessen Mission es ist, Menschen auf Befehl zu töten, zu „terminieren".

ice-skating and ballet lessons. A girl would read novels and stories, not old encyclopaedias from skips. A girl would want to learn French knitting and the recorder and how to make a cake (that bit might be difficult). In fact, a girl would want the childhood that June had once had, the one she had despised so much when she became a teenager. Would her daughter grow up and treat her the way June treated her own mother? That would be ironic, wouldn't it, like punishment fitting the crime. The baby gave her a double punch, right upper cut, left hook. Perhaps it wouldn't be the kind of girl that June imagined. That would serve her right too.

She conceived Eddie on holiday. Things had never been the same for June after she terminated that foetus. She'd been top of her class at Watson's before but afterwards she lost interest in academic achievement. She'd limped on to the end of school and gone on holiday to Greece with a group of friends from her class. To Crete, although she'd never been sure where that was on the map. Eddie knew where it was on the map because he'd asked her, straight out, 'Where was I conceived?' She'd caught him reading one of her baby books (she wished she could get Hawk to read one). It

Stricken mit einer Strickliesel • Blockflöte • verachtet hatte • eine dem Verbrechen angemessene Strafe • doppelt • Boxhieb • Aufwärtshaken • Haken • empfing • (Name der Schule) • Erfolg • hatte sich … geschleppt • Kreta

Übung 5

In der Buchstabenschlange sind die englischen Übersetzungen folgender Wörter versteckt, allerdings nicht in dieser Reihenfolge:

Strafe, verachten, Kreta, Bänder, Erfolg, büßen, flechten.

Markieren Sie die versteckten Wörter.

naoceribbonsnanxodespisenmuopsgxayatoneyupsvietnh
symcreteclemystawipisympunishmentqopjefmtuclwpom
eruhpoqplaitxvnhgorutrommsamwoachievementyartuvo

seemed unnatural for a boy of his age to be interested in things like that. June wondered if it was a sign that he was gay. She wouldn't mind if he was, it was neither here nor there, she was all for gays – the more the better in fact – as long as it didn't make his life more difficult than it already was.

fragte sich • schwul • es spielte keine Rolle

Eddie had been reading June's baby books. He thought it was odd that women had to read books to know how to be a mother, although he could see that his own mother needed a bit of a hand. He was looking forward to helping with the baby. If he helped with her she would love him even more. And he'd be a big brother, a hero to her. He liked the idea of being a hero.
He supposed she had been conceived in his mother's big, never-made bed. He knew the mechanics of it and he could hear them at it all the time. It had obviously never struck his mother that if she could say 'Eddie, come in here' from her bedroom without raising her voice and he could hear her in his own bedroom (although he usually pretended he couldn't), then it was more than likely that he was also going to hear her when she was yelling her head off in there going, 'Ohgod, ohgod, ohgod.' It wasn't clever and it wasn't

seltsam • etwas Hilfe brauchte • Held • nie gemacht • war … in den Sinn gekommen • ihre Stimme zu erheben • so tat, als ob • mehr als wahrscheinlich • wie verrückt schrie

info

„Ode on a Grecian Urn" ist ein Gedicht des englischen Lyrikers John Keats (1795–1821), einem der wichtigsten Vertreter der englischen Romantik. Zunächst studierte er Medizin, obwohl er sich immer schon mehr für die Poesie interessierte. 1817 veröffentlichte er seinen ersten Gedichtband „Poems". 1819 schrieb Keats mehrere Oden, die als die vollendetsten und makellosesten seiner Werke gelten.
Ode bezeichnet ursprünglich ein lyrisches Strophengedicht der Antike, später dann feierliche, oft reimlose lyrische Dichtung in kunstvollem Stil.

funny, as Mrs McFarlane, his English teacher, would have said.

Eddie, on the other hand, had been conceived on the island of Crete, which was Greek and in the Mediterranean and to which he hoped to sail one day on a fast wooden boat with a white sail like a wing. He had a book called an *Ancient Greek Primer* which he'd found in a jumble sale, but if he'd thought Latin was difficult then Greek took the biscuit, as his grandmother would have said. But it was beautiful to look at. They had done 'Ode on a Grecian Urn*' in English, which had proved a bit too advanced for them, as Mrs McFarlane herself had admitted, but not before breaking down in tears, although that was probably because of her divorce rather than the Grecian Urn, but he had remembered the thing about beauty and truth because it seemed profound, which was his word of the week.

Tammy lay on her back with her legs in the air while he tickled her huge stomach. She looked as if she was going to burst any minute. He'd had to get a book out of the library on dogs because it didn't look as if either Hawk or his mother was going to make an effort to find out about whatever the word for dogs was. Puppybirth. Ha ha ha.

Another parents' evening. Surely one a year was enough. June found schools oppressive, all those female teachers looking at her, wondering how old she was when she had Eddie, judging her. It was such a schemie school. She wished she could afford to live somewhere better, send Eddie to a good school. His life would be different (his future would be different) if he went somewhere like Watson's, the teachers would take more interest in him, care about him more. At least a few more of the teachers knew who Eddie was now. 'Eddie's developing quite a personality,' his science teacher said. What did that mean? 'Eddie,' his maths teacher ruminated, 'he's quite the comedian, isn't he?'

Mittelmeer

(Alte griechische Fibel) • Trödelmarkt • schoss den Vogel ab

Scheidung

tiefsinnig

kitzelte

beklemmend • voller Schüler aus ärmlichen Verhältnissen • sich leisten

grübelte • Komiker

(It was *never* good when they said that.) 'Eddie never seems to be quite *with* us,' the French teacher said, 'but he's pleasant enough.'

'Are you all right?' his English teacher asked her. She made a sympathetic face at June, cocking her head on one side and smiling at her. 'I can get you a cup of tea, if you want?' she offered. 'I remember how tiring it is when you're carrying such a weight around.' It took June a second to realize she meant the baby. June had left her contacts out and she squinted to see the English teacher's name on the handwritten sign in front of her. 'No thanks, Mrs … McFarlane.' June felt about six years old. 'Oh, call me Pam,' the English teacher said cheerfully, 'everyone else does,' and June felt glad that 'Pam' was one of Eddie's teachers because she seemed the caring sort, but then she saw that little frown pinching her round maternal features as she said, 'Eddie …' and June could see that she couldn't remember which one he was.

Despite her plump, mumsy look, she had a neurotic air about her – exactly the kind of woman June had always dreaded turning into. 'One minute they're a bump,' Mrs McFarlane laughed, 'and the next minute they're huge teenagers. And then they're gone.' She leant across the table in a conspiratorial way. June shrank back. 'Make the most of every day,' 'Pam' said. 'Every day is precious.'

'Yeah, right,' June said.

June couldn't imagine Eddie leaving home. He was days away from his twelfth birthday. Every time Eddie had a birthday June tried – and usually failed – to disguise the fact that he had hardly any relatives and no friends at all. In order to increase his pathetic tally of cards, even June's mother sent him two birthday cards, one from herself and one, written with her left hand, from an anonymous, mysterious admirer, the same one who sent him a Valentine* every year.

June was sure that Eddie would never win a fist

scheint nie richtig dabei zu sein • soweit ganz nett • mitfühlend • Miene • legte ihren Kopf schief

Kontaktlinsen • blinzelte

fröhlich

Stirnrunzeln • zwickte • mütterlich • Gesichtszüge • füllig • matronenhaft • hatte ein … Auftreten • befürchtet hatte • kleine Beule (früher Schwangerenbauch) • riesig • verschwörerisch • wich zurück • kostbar • Verwandte • zu vergrößern • Strichliste • anonym • Verehrerin • Valentinsgruß

fight, never have a good job and never receive a Valentine from anyone other than his grandmother. And it would all be her fault somehow. She imagined him when she was dead – a solitary middle-aged man ('pleasant enough') living in a stained and soiled flat, obsessively collecting newspapers and cereal packets.

The American flagfish – *Jordanella floridae*. A good name for a girl, Eddie thought. 'Oh yes, and may I introduce my girlfriend, Miss Jordanella Floridae?' He chortled. His nearly adolescent antennae sensed his mother watching disapprovingly from the doorway and he deliberately picked his nose to annoy her. He was looking forward to having a girlfriend, he knew he'd end up with a geeky one but he didn't mind. They'd be pals, the way he was going to be pals with his invisible sister.

June regarded Eddie with despair. He was sitting cross-legged in the middle of the carpet, bent almost double over an old book and cackling maniacally to himself. The new baby fluttered inside her, elbowing more room for itself. June wanted to tell Eddie that

Schuld
voller Flecken • verschmutzt • Frühstücksflocken • Floridakärpfling
gluckste • jugendlich • missbilligend • absichtlich • bohrte … in der Nase • Kumpel
tief über … gebeugt • gackerte • wie verrückt • bewegte sich unruhig

info

In England und den USA ist es besonders unter Jugendlichen Brauch, der oder dem Angehimmelten am Valentinstag eine Karte zu schicken, die oft nicht unterzeichnet ist. Natürlich hofft der Absender, dass die oder der Angeschriebene errät, von wem die Karte kommt. Je mehr Karten jemand erhält, desto beliebter ist er vermeintlich. Der Valentinstag wird am 14. Februar gefeiert – ursprünglich zu Ehren des heiligen Valentin, Bischof von Terni, der der Legende nach an diesem Tag im Jahr 269 hingerichtet worden sein soll. Er gilt als Schutzpatron der Liebenden und Verlobten. Heute beschenken an diesem Tag vor allem Männer ihre Frauen mit Blumen.

she loved him but instead she said, 'Don't pick your nose, Eddie.'

'Do I look like my father?' he asked when she had already left the room. 'I can't remember what he looked like,' she shouted from the hallway. Which was more or less true. He didn't often ask but when he did she always said his father was 'some guy she met on holiday'. Which was also more or less true.

'What do you want to do for your birthday, squirt?' Hawk asked. Hawk was staring at the table in front of him on which the innards of a barometer, acquired at a car boot sale, were laid out in a way that suggested they would never go back together again.

'Deep Sea World,' Eddie replied instantly.

'Again?'

'Again.'

Flur
im Urlaub
Würstchen
Innereien • erstanden • (eine Art) Flohmarkt • vermuten ließ • (das größte Meeresaquarium in Schottland)

✶

'Oh, not again.' June sighed as they headed out across the Forth Road Bridge in Hawk's tinny old van. She was doing her best, but she felt sick. 'It's the fourth time this year, Eddie.'

'It's *my* birthday, I get to choose,' Eddie said cheerfully.

blechern • Lieferwagen

Übung 6

Lösen Sie das Kreuzworträtsel mithilfe der folgenden Erklärungen:

Down

1 away from one's own country

2 a woman trained to help women in childbirth

3 a small truck used especially for transporting goods

4 insect with large wings, often with beautiful colours

Across

5 made from a soft metal

6 a corridor

'We could have gone to Butterfly World,' June said, more to herself than anyone. The baby would like Butterfly World. A girl who would like butterflies. Hawk's van smelt of wet dog as they drove across the Forth Road Bridge, the water grey beneath their wheels.

(Freizeitpark in Edinburgh) • Schmetterlinge

June didn't like the sea. She had done once but not after Crete. It had been her first holiday abroad – her parents had never been comfortable with the idea of foreign holidays, they contained too many potential hazards. There were four of them – two boys, Andy and Mark, herself and a girl called Joanna, who was a midwife now (June had seen her at the antenatal clinic), which you would never have thought would be her fate if you'd met her then.

They had taken a little boat out onto that vast expanse of azure as different from the Firth of Forth as was possible and when they were a long way from shore they all decided to go swimming off the boat. They'd been drinking retsina and smoking dope after a big lunch of oily moussaka and green beans (her father would have said they were going out of their way to die) but they were all reckless, or maybe they all thought they were immortal. June wasn't sure that she thought at all at that age.

im Ausland • beinhalteten • Gefahren • Hebamme • Schwangerenberatung • Azurblau • (Meeresarm an der Ostküste von Schottland) • Retsina (griechischer Weißwein) • Marihuana • gaben sich große Mühe • unbekümmert • unsterblich

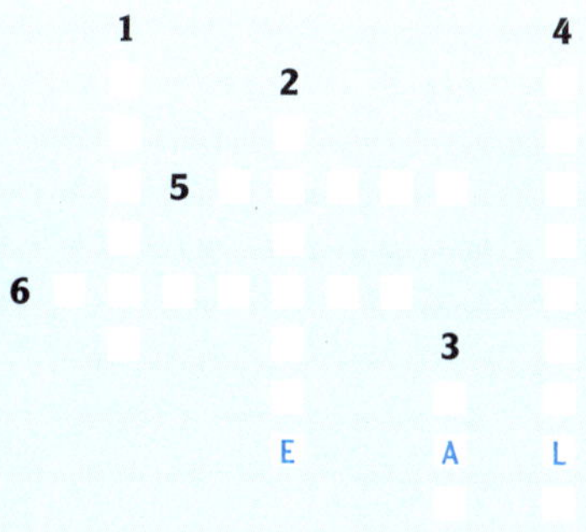

June was a strong swimmer – her parents had made sure she could swim as drowning was always high on their list of likely ways to die – and she had loved the feeling of kicking out in all that warm water with the sun like a bronze mirror in the sky, beating down on her back. They had seen flying silver fish and a school of dolphins before they dived in the water and June was hoping that one of the dolphins would come back and find her. She had seen a mosaic once, in some Roman villa on one of the sunless British holidays her parents took her on, and in the mosaic a boy was riding on a dolphin's back, and June thought if she could do that, if she could ride on a dolphin, she would be happy. And if she could actually turn into a dolphin, then she might be happy for ever.

At first she thought that maybe it was a dolphin that took her down because, without any warning, she found herself being dragged abruptly to the bottom of the Mediterranean. Straight down, not the floundering, bubbling chaos of cramp or tiredness, but a speeding, rushing drop as if an anchor had been tied to her feet. And the odd thing was, when she arrived on the seabed, stepping lightly off the rock she had landed on as if getting off a bus, she could still breathe.

Ertrinken

Delfinschwarm

römisch

sich in … verwandeln

gezogen • zappelnd • blubbernd • Krampf • rasend • Sinken • Anker • Meeresgrund

Übung 7 Welche Aussagen stimmen? Kreuzen Sie sie an.

June was good at swimming.
She had once seen a painting of a dolphin in a Roman villa.
June would have liked to turn into a dolphin.
She slowly sank to the seabed.
June's parents were afraid their daughter might drown.
Her parents only went on holiday with her in Great Britain.
June discovered an anchor on the seabed.
June was on a little boat in the Atlantic.

She could remember seeing shells and fish, squid and crabs, she could remember the sunlight on the surface, a long way above her head. She could even remember how it felt to glide as effortlessly as a water nymph through the sea, but after that everything was confused in her memory and what happened next was so very rich and strange that she thought that someone must have given her acid. Certainly dropping acid was the only logical explanation she could come up with afterwards for the underwater kingdom – the massive throne of green marble decorated with gold and red coral and mother-of-pearl and cushioned with sealskin, the sea beasts that swam around like lap dogs, the massive white horses whose manes were huge waves endlessly breaking around their heads as they pawed the sand, impatient to be harnessed to his chariot. And only some serious psychotropic drug could have accounted for his colossal, roaring presence of which she seemed only to catch fragments – the disgusting smell of fish and whale fat, the fronds of seaweed entangled in his great beard, his seed like pearls, gushing into the blue water–

'You all right?' Hawk asked her.

'Fine,' June said.

'What shall we call the baby?' Eddie asked from the back of the van and June's heart gave a little flap at the word 'we'. June and Eddie. June and Eddie and the baby. A family. She wanted to squash Eddie to her breast. Instead she said, 'Close your mouth, Eddie. If the wind changes you'll stay like that.'

June knew that Eddie liked everything in Deep Sea World but that the thing he liked most was the Underwater Safari – the moving walkway in the huge acrylic-that-looked-like-glass tunnel that took you down, down, right into the kingdom of fishes, from the forests of sunlit kelp where the little fish darted, to the sandy flats where the skate hid on the bottom, to the depths of the abyss where the scary conger eels

Tintenfische • Krabben • Oberfläche • mühelos • Wassernymphe

LSD (= Droge) • einwerfen

Marmor • Korallen • Perlmutt • Seehundsfell • Schoßhunde • scharrten • vor … gespannt zu werden • Triumphwagen • Psychopharmakon • konnte für … verantwortlich gewesen sein • Wedel • verheddert • sprudelnd • Schlag • drücken

Seetang • umherschossen • Rochen • Abgrund • Seeaale

lurked, to the open ocean with its shimmering silver fish. June was convinced that the weight of the water would break the tunnel and they would all be swept away on a North Sea tsunami of cod and salmon and sea bass. She reminded herself to think happy thoughts for the sake of the baby.

davongespült würden • Kabeljau • Lachs • Wolfsbarsch • um … willen •

Someone called Jamie had a birthday today. Eddie knew that because there was a handwritten sign stuck up in the tunnel amongst the seaweed fronds, a sign that said 'Happy Seventh Birthday, Jamie'. Eddie didn't suppose anyone had done the same for him but that didn't stop him hoping.

ragte heraus • inmitten

nahm nicht an, dass

'Shite,' June said when she saw the happy birthday sign. 'Shite, shite, shite.' Why didn't she know you could do that? Because she was a crap mother, obviously. She imagined how happy Eddie would have been if he'd had a sign. She felt sick again.

Scheiße

Scheiß-

Afterwards, they ate in the cafeteria, an indifferent meal of chips and baked beans because it seemed wrong to eat fish. It was wet and windy outside and so cold that for once Hawk's van felt warm. June wanted a cigarette. Surely the baby wouldn't mind just one cigarette?

mittelmäßig • Pommes frites • weiße Bohnen in Tomatensoße

Going home, they got stuck halfway across the bridge in a rush-hour traffic jam. Hawk drummed a tuneless tune on the steering wheel. The water beneath was a wretched steel colour with a curdled froth on the wind-whipped waves. June wondered how long they would survive in the water if the suspension cables snapped.

blieben … stecken • Verkehrsstau • Lenkrad • erbärmlich • geronnen • Gischt • Aufhängungsseile • rissen

Eddie had his nose pressed to the back window of the van. The rain had cleared behind them, bathing Fife in a watery gold sun. Down in the water Eddie could see mermaids leaping out of the river like salmon, their goldfish tails catching the sun. Nereids sun-

(Grafschaft in Schottland) • Meerjungfrauen • Nereiden

bathed on Inchcolm Island while a huge shoal of silver fish whirled the Forth into a vortex in obeisance to their secret god – Eddie, King of the Fish. 'Thank you, loyal subjects,' Eddie said, giving a regal wave to the inhabitants of his watery realm.

'Don't talk to yourself, Eddie,' June said. 'It's the first sign of madness.'

Schwarm • (Fluss) • Strudel • Ehrerbietung • majestätisch • (König-) • Reich

June wondered if Hawk would hang around long enough to see the baby born. She wished he would leave now instead of putting her through the misery of waiting for him to go. Hawk himself was thinking that he fancied joining a tepee community. The baby inside June wasn't thinking at all, it was leaping for the joy of leaping.

Eddie laughed to himself because he, and only he, knew what the great blue and white marbled carp had said to him that day in the Botanics.

Eddie leant forward and put his small, hot, dirty hand into June's hand and said, 'Everything's going to be OK, Mum. Trust me.'

Misere

damit liebäugelte • sich … anzuschließen • Tipi

Vertrau mir.

Übung 8

Setzen Sie die Verben in der richtigen Form ein – simple oder progressive form – und achten Sie dabei auf die richtige Zeit.

1. ____________ (to stick up) amongst the plants was a handwritten sign.
2. Eddie knew the sign was not there for him, but nevertheless he couldn't stop ______________ (to hope).
3. She told herself ______________ (to think) positively for the sake of her baby.
4. The island was ___________ (to bathe) in golden sunlight.
5. Hawk fancied ___________ (to join) a special community.

Nunc scio quid sit amor.

VIRGIL

Sheer Big Waste of Love

Addison Fox was named for his father. Bill Addison refused to have anything to do with his unlooked-for son but Addison's mother, Shirley, was determined to get Addison's father's name on his birth certificate, one way or another. Addison met his father only once, when he was seven years old – an encounter so traumatic (Addison, his mother and a relatively innocent bystander ended up in the casualty department of the local hospital) that Addison lost any further desire to be acquainted with his reluctant father.

Paternity, in general, wasn't a subject that Addison had ever given much thought to until he found that he was going to be a father himself. When he celebrated his fortieth birthday Addison had neither child nor wife. When he celebrated his forty-first he had both, one inside the other. Every morning when Addison woke up he was surprised anew by these two facts.

Addison had been courted, bedded and wedded in haste by a primary-school teacher called Clare Soutar. Addison met her when he gave her a speeding ticket on the M8. Addison never did understand how she had got his phone number out of him (it was against so many rules it didn't bear thinking about) but he seemed to remember that it was some ruse about coming to her school to give a talk to the children about what it was like to be a traffic policeman.

Clare, Addison very soon discovered, ran her entire life at breakneck speed. By the time they were sprinting up the aisle he had begun to wonder if she didn't have some kind of metabolic disease. 'Well, neither of us are getting any younger, Addison,' she said, when she proposed to him after two months of hectic dating.

ungewollt • Geburtsurkunde • irgendwie • Begegnung • unbeteiligt • Zuschauer • Unfallstation • Kontakt zu haben mit • widerwillig • Vaterschaft • von Neuem • war umworben worden • ins Bett geholt • vermählt • in Eile • Grundschul- • Strafzettel für Geschwindigkeitsüberschreitung • dass man gar nicht darüber nachdenken durfte • Trick • Verkehrspolizist • halsbrecherisch • Stoffwechselkrankheit • ihm einen Heiratsantrag machte

Umwerben • aufkleben • illustriert • Stiele von Eis am Stiel • Pappröhren • Küchenpapierrollen • Schauspiele • Seelenwanderung • um nur drei Dinge zu nennen • Kapitelle

unbedeutendes Mitglied der königlichen Familie • Pasteten (Wortspiel zu volutes) • glaubte • umgangen • an der es ihm fehlte

Addison spent several evenings of their early courtship helping with lesson preparation. At the time, Clare had been doing a project on the Ancient Greeks with her Primary Sevens – cutting and pasting pictorial maps of a Greek city state, constructing a Trojan horse out of ice-lolly sticks, making chitons* out of sheets and temples out of the cardboard tubes from kitchen rolls, and mounting dramatic little playlets about the adventures of the gods. Addison learnt a lot from this project – geometry, epic poetry, metempsychosis, to name but three things – and wondered how he had lived all his life in Edinburgh without knowing anything about Greek columns*. 'Doric*, Ionic*, Corinthian*,' he explained to his partner, Robbie, one afternoon as they crawled up the Mound*, escorting a car containing some minor royal, 'take the National Gallery* for example, the volutes* on that are–' until Robbie told him that he really didn't give a shite what the vol-au-vents on the National Gallery were. Addison reckoned that if he stuck with Clare he might make up for the education he had mysteriously bypassed at an earlier age. If he was lucky, he thought, he might make up for some of the mothering he lacked as well.

info

Ein **Chiton** ist ein antikes griechisches Unterkleid, das gewickelt und an den Schultern mit Spangen gehalten wird.
Das **Kapitell** ist der obere Abschluss einer Säule oder eines Pfeilers. Es gibt viele verschiedene Ausformungen des Kapitells. In der griechischen Architektur werden drei Haupttypen unterschieden, die sich vor allem in der Art der Verzierung voneinander unterscheiden: **dorisch**, **ionisch** und **korinthisch**.
The Mound ist ein künstlich aufgeschütteter Hügel in Schottlands Hauptstadt Edinburgh. Er verbindet die „old town" mit der „new town". Auf ihm befinden sich einige wichtige Gebäude wie

Clare herself was from a family that was top-heavy with competent maternal women. Her mother was a district nurse, one sister, Fiona, was an assistant bank manager, another, Kirsty, a social worker. Clare's father was a meek, bemused man who submitted willingly to female authority. 'Best just to give in to them,' he confided to Addison, over his first family dinner, 'makes for a much easier life.'

'Clare's always liked a man in uniform,' her mother said to Addison.

'Oh yeah,' Fiona laughed casually, 'she's had a fireman, that guy that was in the navy, even that history lecturer was in the TA*, wasn't he?'

'A sergeant in the traffic division's a good one, though,' Kirsty said, as if Addison was part of a set to be collected.

Addison stared at his plate of pork casserole and mashed potatoes and felt slightly sick.

'He's sitting right in front of you,' Clare rebuked mildly and she caught Addison's eye and winked at him. It struck him that he knew absolutely nothing about family life. He supposed this was something else he was going to have to learn.

It was only when Clare was drawing up the seating plan

voller • Gemeindeschwester • sanftmütig • ratlos • sich unterordnete • nachzugeben • vertraute … an • beiläufig • Marine • Geschichtsdozent • Wachtmeister • Auflauf mit Schweinefleisch • Kartoffelbrei • leicht • tadelte • stellte mit … Blickkontakt her • zwinkerte … zu • mit einem Schlag wurde ihm klar • Sitzordnung

die „Royal Scottish Academy", die „Bank of Scotland" und die **National Gallery**. Das nationale Kunstmuseum befindet sich in einem klassizistischen Bau. Die Gemäldesammlung umfasst vor allem schottische und europäische Werke.

Voluten sind schnecken- bzw. spiralförmige Verzierungen von Bauelementen, häufig an Kapitellen oder Giebeln zu finden.

TA steht für Territorial Army; sie besteht aus freiwilligen Reservisten, die sich ihren Lebensunterhalt in einem anderen Beruf verdienen.

for the church that Addison's truly remarkable absence of relatives became apparent to her. They had been so busy getting to know each other in the details (a shared hatred of mushrooms, a love of fairground rides and so on) that the bigger things (Addison's orphan status, Clare's diabetes) had got slightly overlooked.

'No one at all?' she frowned. Addison shook his head. 'Not even a second cousin three times removed?'

No one, he assured her. Which was a lie, but it was so much easier than the truth. Addison simplified his life story for Clare – he had been illegitimate (a fact borne out by his birth certificate), his mother died the week before his eighth birthday, when no one came forward to claim him he had been sent to a vicious Catholic orphanage where he had stayed until his sixteenth birthday. At the age of twenty he decided he had a choice between following a life of crime or becoming a policeman, and had chosen the latter. He was a beat sergeant before transferring to traffic where he had served six out of the seven years he was allowed. When he left traffic he was hoping to become a dog handler. He liked dogs, he didn't like traffic. After six years he thought it was normal to die in a car crash. Addison didn't think it was healthy to think like that.

Fehlen von • geteilt • starke Abneigung gegen • Pilze • Jahrmarkt • Fahrgeschäfte • Waisen- • unehelich • die durch … bestätigt wurde • um Anspruch auf ihn zu erheben • bösartig • Waisenhaus • Letzteres • Streifenpolizist • Hundeführer

info

Der Rotary Club ist eine weltweit agierende, unabhängige und überparteiliche Organisation von mehr als 1,2 Millionen Männern und Frauen, die in ihrem Beruf, in Wirtschaft und Kommune in führender Weise tätig sind. Getreu ihrem Motto „selbstloses Dienen" besteht das Hauptziel der in örtlichen Clubs organisierten Rotarierinnen und Rotarier darin, überall in der Welt gemeinnützige Arbeit zu leisten. Man kann nicht beschließen, Mitglied zu werden, man kann nur zum Mitglied ernannt werden. Dafür muss man gute Charaktereigenschaften und einen guten Ruf besitzen und sich auch im Beruf bewährt haben. Man muss sich zudem verpflichten, am Clubleben aktiv teilzunehmen.

'And your mother,' Clare said, puzzled, 'she never said who your father was?'
'Never,' Addison said.

✶

Shirley talked about Addison's father a lot. 'Your father' she would say to Addison, in a way that sounded oddly formal. Bill Addison had been a fighter pilot who after the war had turned his mechanic's hand to cars, starting with a modest garage on the A1 on the way out of Edinburgh and building to a small empire dotted all around the city. For a brief period – in his self-penned advertising material – he was known as the Car King.
Occasionally, Bill Addison's photograph would appear in the paper – a Rotary Club* dinner or the opening of a new garage – and Shirley would cut it out and keep it on the kitchen table – where most things were kept – and would brood over it for days before eventually tearing it up in a fit of bitterness and burning it on the fire. In the absence of any real facts from Shirley, Addison developed his own version of his father. A handsome war hero – Addison knew the type from comics – still fighting a war somewhere (despite the Rotary Club dinners) and thus unable to return to his loving wife and son. Addison imagined him high in the clouds, like a god in his chariot, overseeing all his son did. One day he would drive up their street in a golden car (possibly with a crown on his head) and whisk them away to a much better life.
Addison eavesdropped for additional information, for whenever Shirley's friend Mary came round in the evening to help Shirley work her way down to the bottom of a bottle of gin, the conversation would inevitably turn to Addison's paternity. 'Ha,' he heard his mother say once, 'he came in a fucking shower of gold,' and Mary said, 'I hope you made him pay extra,'

verwundert

Kampfpilot • Händchen für Motoren • bescheiden • verstreut • selbst verfasst • Werbematerial

brütete … darüber • schließlich • zerriss • in einem Anfall von • gut aussehend

Krone • entführen • lauschte • zusätzlich

Goldregen

and they both howled with laughter and choked on their cigarettes and gin. Another time, Mary (who seemed to know his father almost as well as Shirley did) complained that Bill Addison didn't think he was subject to the same rules as 'mere mortals'.

'Aye,' Shirley agreed, 'his sort always gets away with it.'

✶

The wedding was like a school project on a large scale and Clare and her family approached it with an efficiency and economy that would have been sorely coveted by Addison's chief inspector. Addison was dragged round the stalls of one wedding fair after another by Clare and forced to help her choose 'favour baskets' and 'colour-coordinated balloons' and God knows what other stuff he had never suspected existed. She cut articles from bridal magazines with titles like 'Ways To Panic Proof Your Wedding' and 'Ten Things To Consider Before You Say I Do' and Addison had begun to think that the strategic-planning stage would go on for ever when suddenly he found himself standing at the altar wondering if she would see sense and jilt him at the last minute.

It was a church wedding even though Clare was a professed atheist, something she refrained from telling the Church of Scotland minister. There was a fast and furious ceilidh at the reception and Addison was introduced to more Soutars than he thought it was possible for one country to contain.

Before he knew it, the wedding was over and they were on a plane bound for some Greek island the name of which Addison had missed. When Addison woke up on the first morning of his honeymoon he felt completely disorientated, as if he had been on a long journey through space and time and had been dropped back down to earth into another life altogether. A life where

brachen in brüllendes Gelächter aus • verschluckten sich an • Normalsterbliche • kommt damit davon • im großen Maßstab • gingen … an • die bei … äußerst begehrt gewesen wäre • Hauptkommissar • Stände • Hochzeitsmesse • Geschenkkörbchen • Brautzeitschriften • die zu bedenken sind • „Ich will“ • ihm den Laufpass geben würde • bekennend • unterließ … zu • (die Staatskirche in Schottland) • Pfarrer • Unterhaltungsabend mit Musik und Gedichtvorträgen • unterwegs zu • Flitterwochen • vollkommen

an unknown woman was snoring gently next to him in a bed that was on fire with foreign sunlight.
His own mother had never had a honeymoon or a wedding, never been a bride or a wife. Shirley had been a prostitute. He didn't tell Clare this, not because he was ashamed, Addison knew no woman walked the streets from anything less than dire necessity, but because he thought it was no one's business other than Shirley's. What puzzled Addison, given the nature of his mother's profession, was why his mother had been so grimly certain about the source of his paternity.
Only with hindsight did Addison understand the reason for his one and only visit to his father. His mother must have known she was dying and she had been trying to find another home for her only child. When he thought about this it made him feel unbearably sad, not for himself, but for his mother.

schnarchte • sanft

Prostituierte • sich schämte • dringlich • Notwendigkeit

eisern • seiner Abstammung • rückblickend • einzig

unerträglich

*

Addison and his mother caught a bus and travelled to the other side of Edinburgh, where the broad, tree-lined streets and the big houses with their abundant

nahmen

üppig

Übung 9

Vervollständigen Sie die folgenden Sätze mit den passenden Präpositionen: with – into – by – for – from – in – at – of (Achtung, zwei Präpositionen werden nicht benötigt).

1. Some people get away ________ almost everything.
2. Only now could Addison understand the reason ________ his visit to his father many years ago.
3. Though Clare didn't believe ________ God, she refrained ________ letting the minister know.
4. Addison found himself standing ________ the altar.
5. He had the strange feeling he had been dropped ________ a totally different life.

Griff • besorgt • Ängstlichkeit • Launen • der Hauptstadt • Hochgefühl • gehässig • Böswilligkeit • nach draußen zu huschen • herumlungerte • war … Experte im • Ewigkeit • stiegen … aus • Überfluss • Blüte • wohl • beruhigend • Handrasenmäher • hell klingend • Gerüche • ebenso • frisch gemäht • Flieder

summer gardens seemed to Addison to belong to a quite different city from the one where he lived, in a dark tenement in which you could smell the docks but not see the water.

His mother had started off the journey in good spirits but was soon in the grip of a fretful anxiety. Shirley's moods were as changeable as the capital's weather and she could move from wild elation to spiteful malevolence in the time it took Addison to scurry out into the security of the street where he would loiter until it seemed safe to go home. By the age of five Addison was adept at loitering.

After what seemed an eternity to Addison, they finally alighted from the bus. He was disappointed to discover that they hadn't arrived at their destination and still had an endless walk down several more of those broad, treelined streets. Addison wondered who it was that lived amongst this opulence of blossom trees and how his mother could possibly know them.

It was a Sunday and the air was full of noises that were foreign to Addison's ears – the soothing rhythm of push-and-pull lawnmowers and the clarion call of church bells. The scents of a Sunday in the suburbs were equally exotic – new-mown grass, lilacs and the

Übung 10 Welche der jeweils drei Möglichkeiten ist die richtige? Streichen Sie die falschen durch.

1. As a young boy, Addison was always lonely. / angry. / hungry.

2. A teacher / neighbour / saleswoman often gave Addison something to eat.

3. Shirley used to wear shoes which were dirty. / with very high heels. / with delicate patterns.

tantalizing aroma of roasting meat. Addison was very hungry. Addison was always hungry. Shirley's idea of breakfast was a slice hacked off a white loaf, scraped with margarine and sprinkled with sugar. Sometimes she didn't even remember that, and Addison had to make do with the small bottle of playground milk at school break-time. If Shirley forgot to feed him at the weekend or in the school holidays then Addison could go hungry all day, although, often as not, one of the women in the street where he lived would throw him down a jeelie piece or a sixpence for a poke of chips. Addison was called 'the poor wee wean' more often than he was ever called Addison.

This morning a restless, festive mood had led Shirley to buy lardy Aberdeen rolls from the corner shop but she had rushed Addison to the bus stop before he'd had time to tear off more than one mouthful.

Addison began to lag behind. The steel tips of his mother's stiletto heels made a brutish noise on the street. All Shirley's shoes were the same – sharply pointed at the toe and with heels that were precariously, ludicrously high. She was forever staggering and turning her ankle or tripping on cracks in the pavement and if she wanted to run for the bus she had

verlockend • bratend • Scheibe • abgehackt von • Brotlaib • beschmiert mit • bestreut mit • musste sich mit … begnügen • meistens • (= jelly) Marmeladenbrot • (Geldstück) • Tüte • kleines Baby • fettig • (schottische Brötchenspezialität) • zurückzubleiben • Stahlspitzen • gefährlich • aberwitzig • taumelte • stolperte • Ritzen

good spirits.
4. Shirley had started off the journey in deep thought.
a special mood.
on a Sunday.

5. They went to his father's house on his birthday.
on a Wednesday.
go to his grandparents a lot.

6. As a boy, Addison used to hang around in the streets.
stay at home most of the time.

to take her shoes off and sprint in her stockinged feet. When she died, a year later, Addison could remember his mother's shoes long after he'd forgotten her face. Shirley yanked him by the hand, 'Come *on*, Addison,' she said, and Addison heard the tetchy note in her voice that meant it would be best for him to trot along as fast as possible.

Eventually, they came to a halt in front of a tall wrought-iron gate. Shirley lit a nervous cigarette and alternated between smoking it and chewing her lip while staring at the gate, lost in agitated thought. Addison had once heard a neighbour refer to his mother as 'highly strung' and although he had no idea what that meant he knew it sounded like an uncomfortable thing to be.

As if she'd come to a decision, Shirley threw the half-smoked cigarette down and ground it into the pavement with the sole of one pointed shoe. She checked her make-up and her hair in her compact mirror and straightened the little jacket she was wearing over her smartest dress – a striped shirtwaister with three-quarter sleeves and a stiff collar that had been fashionable several years before Addison's birth. Addison always thought of his mother as a young woman and

in Strümpfen
zerrte … an • reizbar • nebenherzutraben
schmiedeeisern
aufgewühlt • als … bezeichnete • überspannt
Puderdose • glättete • Hemdblusenkleid • steif • Kragen • in Mode • mehrere

Übung 11 Ordnen Sie den untenstehenden Substantiven folgende Adjektive sinnvoll zu: **wrought-iron** – **booming** – **agitated** – **stiff** – **melodious** – **striped**

a ____________________ voice
a ____________________ gate
in ____________________ thought
a ____________________ dress
a ____________________ collar
____________________ laughter

was surprised when many years later he realized that she was forty when she died, only a year younger than Addison was now. She was a drinker, of course, and, although the drink didn't kill her, it didn't help to stop the cancer already racing round her body on that summer Sunday morning.

She snapped the compact shut. 'Right,' she said, to herself rather than Addison. She swung open the wrought-iron gate and walked briskly up the path, her heels striking like flints off the slabs of York stone, but her purposefulness seemed to evaporate when she reached the front door, where she stopped, looking suddenly forlorn, like someone who had been locked out rather than someone who was trying to get in. 'Christ, Addison,' she muttered to him as if he were a fellow adult, 'I could do with a fucking drink.'

The door was a massy, ornate affair in heavily varnished wood and it reminded Addison of the bank in town that his mother took him to sometimes. Shirley, as with many other things in her life, went into the bank with high hopes and invariably came out with them dashed. She would enquire of one of the blank-faced cashiers in a tight, strained voice – a sorry attempt at refinement – as to whether any money had 'come into her account' and when the answer was no (Addison had never known it to be yes), she would storm out, ranting and cursing in a language that passers-by seemed to find shocking beyond belief, although it sounded fairly run-of-the-mill to Addison's ears.

Shirley tilted her head to one side as if listening out for something. Unconsciously, Addison imitated her pose. He heard people close by, people who seemed to be enjoying themselves – the booming, bass laughter of a man, the pleasant, melodious voices of women, quite different from Shirley's gravelly smoker's timbre. And, further off, the high notes of children playing, a noise that made Addison perk up like an eager dog.

They followed the thread of voices along a narrow

Krebs • ließ … zuschnappen • forsch • schlugen … auf • Feuersteine • Platten • York-Sandstein • Entschlossenheit • zu verfliegen • verlassen • Herrgott • ebenbürtig • Erwachsener • lackiert • ausnahmslos • zerschlagen • erkundigte sich bei • ausdruckslos • scharf • angespannt • jämmerlich • Versuch • Vornehmheit • Konto • schimpfend • fluchend • unglaublich • ziemlich • alltäglich • neigte • Haltung • dröhnend • heiser • die Ohren spitzen ließ • Klang

stone-chip path that took them round the corner of the pink sandstone wall of the house. The house had a small tower and what looked like battlements and Addison wondered if it was a castle. Shirley hesitated in front of yet another door – a planked wooden one set into a wall. The house might as well have had moat, drawbridge and portcullis for all the difficulties it seemed intent on throwing in her path.

The voices that had lured them were coming from the other side of the wall. Addison heard the clinking of glasses and the ambrosial scent of food. His stomach groaned. 'Sh,' his mother whispered, as if his hunger was something under his control. She gave Addison a critical look and then searched for a handkerchief in her handbag, spat on it, and rubbed Addison's face. She flattened his unruly hair with the palm of her hand, knocking him off balance as she did so. Shirley frowned, unable to see much improvement. She bent down to speak in Addison's ear, an action that made him take an involuntary step backwards.

'Remember,' she cautioned, as if they had discussed the subject beforehand (which Addison was sure they hadn't), 'stand up straight and look him in the eye when he speaks to you. OK?'

'OK,' Addison agreed.

From beyond the wall, there was a sudden burst of laughter as if the punchline of a joke had just been delivered. Shirley took a fortifying breath. 'Right then,' she said, 'time to confront his majesty in all his glory,' and she pushed open the wooden door.

*

There seemed to be a consensus amongst the nuns in the orphanage that Addison's mother was in hell, an idea so horrifying that Addison tried never to think about it. Now, now that the nuns' brainwashing had (more or less) left his system, he knew Shirley was

Ziersplitt

Zinnen

verschalt • Burggraben • Zugbrücke • Fallgatter • entschlossen zu sein • sie angelockt hatten • Klirren • köstlich • knurrte Taschentuch • spuckte darauf • widerspenstig • brachte ihn aus dem Gleichgewicht • unwillkürlich • warnte • zuvor • steh gerade

Ausbruch • Pointe • bestärkend

Übereinkunft • Nonnen

Gehirnwäsche

neither in hell, nor heaven – she was nowhere, she was dead. In some ways he preferred the idea that she was in hell because then at least she would exist.
It was only after Clare's belly began to swell in the months following the wedding ('I'm too old to hang about, Addison') that Addison's own childhood – what little there was of it – began to occupy his mind. If his father had accepted his responsibilities that day, if he had welcomed Addison into his home, how different Addison's life would have been. He would have inhabited a world of golf and dinner-dances and good Edinburgh schools. He would have had brothers and sisters and a sense of belonging to something instead of always feeling like an outsider, an observer of other people's lives. He had thought that having Clare – and now this unknown, unimaginable baby – would change all that. But it didn't. Addison was still on the outside looking in.

Bauch
zu beschäftigen
• Verantwortung
Zugehörigkeitsgefühl • Außenseiter

*

Addison followed his mother and found himself standing on a lawn. Unless you counted the grass on Leith Links, Addison didn't think he'd ever stood on lawn

(öffentliche Parkanlage in Edinburgh)

Übung 12

Vervollständigen Sie die Sätze, indem Sie die Buchstaben in den Klammern in die richtige Reihenfolge bringen.

1. Addison was so hungry that his stomach ____________ (drognea).
2. They had never discussed the ____________ (jsecbtu) beforehand.
3. Clare got pregnant soon after the ____________ (dgwendi).
4. Shirley gave her son a ____________ (litricca) look.
5. Shirley said: "Time to confront his ____________ (mtasjey) in all his glory."

before and his instinct was to kneel down and touch it. Instead, he pressed himself into Shirley's skirts and inhaled her smoky fragrance and silently took in the prospect before them, which, to Addison, looked like a picture from one of his mother's magazines – well-dressed people smoking and drinking and throwing their heads back in easy laughter. The women were sipping delicately from little glasses ('Sherry,' his mother said dismissively under her breath) while the men drank from big cut-glass tumblers.

'Ah, the old amber nectar, Bill,' one of the men said and they touched glasses, making a ringing sound like crystalline bells. Addison regarded 'Bill' with interest. He was a big man, bigger than the others, with the kind of imposing stature that intimidated other men. On the other hand, he didn't seem awfully heroic to Addison – the skin on his cheeks was pouchy and slack and his thinning hair was plastered to his scalp. In contrast, his face sported a huge beard.

There were children racing around the garden, playing a high-spirited game of catch. A boy held a toy aeroplane aloft as he ran and Addison watched its metal wings flashing in the sunshine and wondered if he would be allowed to join in.

niederzuknien • stattdessen • Duft • Aussicht • nippten • vorsichtig • ablehnend • geschliffene • Trinkgläser • bernsteinfarben • kristallen • imponierende • einschüchterte • furchtbar • Wangen • hing sackartig • schlaff • dünner werdend • geklatscht • trug … zur Schau • übermütig • Fangen • in die Höhe • funkelten

Übung 13 Finden Sie die umschriebenen englischen Begriffe und tragen Sie diese in das Kreuzworträtsel ein.

1. extremely
2. hanging loosely
3. to frighten someone
4. a view over a wide area of land or sea
5. having a runny nose
6. Scottish expression for stupid
7. the breaking of a law or rule
8. smelling bad
9. man's hair on the lower part of the face

For all the notice anyone was taking of Addison and his mother they might as well have been cloaked by an invisibility spell. Only one person seemed to see them – a small girl, two or three years old, who was sitting contentedly on a rug on the grass, playing with a doll. When she saw Addison she smiled and waved a clean, plump hand at him, almost as if she'd been expecting him. All the small children of Addison's acquaintance were grubby, snotty, bawling creatures who always smelt rank, but this girl was like a creature from another world. She was wearing a pristine pink dress that spread out around her on the rug like petals and looked as if she smelt of cake and sweets and flowers and other good things that Addison dreamed of.

Addison wondered if she had come from Fairyland – a place Addison knew about because his Primary One teacher, Miss Cameron, had read a story about it to her class (although she had felt it necessary to add the caveat that Fairyland didn't actually exist and was in contravention of all Biblical teaching).

'Don't look so glaikit, Addison,' his mother hissed at him. Afterwards, a long, long time afterwards, Addison came to see this scene for what it was. A family gathered for Sunday lunch, enjoying a pre-prandial

Beachtung, die man … schenkte • hätten … verhüllt sein können • Unsichtbarkeitszauber • zufrieden • Decke • Bekanntenkreis • dreckig • verrotzt • plärrend • ranzig • makellos • Blütenblätter • Märchenland • Vorbehalt • verstieß gegen • (schottisch für) dumm • zusammengekommen zum … • vor dem Essen

Addison wondered if the small girl had come from

1. _ _ f _ _ _ _
2. _ _ a _ _
3. _ _ _ _ _ i _ _ _ _
4. _ r _ _ _ _ _ _
5. _ _ _ _ _ y
6. _ l _ _ _ _ _
7. _ _ _ _ _ a _ _ _ _ _ _ _
8. _ _ n _
9. _ _ _ _ d

drink in the sunshine. At the time, however, it was as if that wooden door had opened on a vision of an unearthly kingdom, peopled by heavenly creatures, and, more than anything he had ever known, Addison wanted to step into that divine world and be a part of it.

A woman appeared at the French windows of the house and came out onto the patio. She was wearing an apron and was holding a wooden spoon in her hand as if she had been tasting something. She called out gaily to the assembled company, 'Lunch is ready, everyone,' but then the cloak of invisibility must have dropped from their shoulders because the woman spotted Addison and Shirley and her hostess smile froze on her lips and her conviviality was replaced by a glacial mask that seemed to Addison to chill the air around him. Still clutching the wooden spoon in one hand, but now brandishing it like a weapon, she called to the little girl ('Susan!') and when Susan didn't respond she hurried to scoop her up protectively, keeping her eyes fixed on Shirley, as if she was a dangerous wild animal that might pounce at any moment. The woman called out sharply to her other children – 'Douglas! Andrew! Pamela!' – and three of the chil-

überirdisch
göttlich
Verandatüren • Terrasse • Schürze • fröhlich • versammelt
entdeckte • gefror • Fröhlichkeit • eisig • abzukühlen • umklammerte • schwang • Waffe • beeilte ... sich • aufzuheben • beschützend • einen Satz machen

Übung 14 Adjektiv oder Adverb – was ist richtig?

1. She called out ________________ (gay/gaily) to everyone to come to dinner.

2. His face didn't show any emotion and looked like a ________________ (glacial/glacially) mask.

3. Shirley was observed as if she was a ________________ (dangerous/dangerously) animal.

4. "This is a private house," Bill said ________________ (angry/angrily) to Shirley.

5. Shirley was advancing on him rather ________________ (aggressive/aggressively).

dren who had been playing catch obediently detached themselves from the others and ran towards their mother. All three were older than Addison. The elder boy still had the toy aeroplane clutched in his hand and Susan, perched against her mother's chest, reached out to grab it. Addison suddenly felt the siren call of cells and DNA and blood and had to resist an almost overwhelming urge to walk across the lawn and shoulder his way into the middle of this little group and become part of Bill Addison's family.

'It's all right, Marjorie,' Bill Addison said, striding across the lawn like a man intent on defending his property. A great cloud passed suddenly over the face of the sun and Addison shivered.

If you ignored the increasingly absurd wooden spoon that Marjorie Addison was holding aloft, she struck an imperious maternal figure. Addison feared that Shirley would stand little chance of victory in any contest with her. There was such cruel fury in her eyes that it seemed to Addison that at any moment she might turn his mother into some helpless creature – a cow or a bear, or worse.

'Now look here,' Bill Addison said angrily to Shirley, 'I don't know what you want, but this is a private house.'

There was a murmur of agreement from the assembled guests. The dark cloud grew darker. Addison felt a drop of rain splash on his cheek.

'You don't know what I want?' Shirley said, her voice cracking with disbelief. Addison saw a streak of lightning fracture the sky and almost immediately thunder banged so loudly that he felt his heart give an answering thump. Susan began to cry. Addison reached for his mother's hand for reassurance but she pulled herself away from him, advancing aggressively on a glowering Bill Addison. Addison followed his mother across the lawn.

'Stop right there, son.' Bill Addison loomed above him, so close that Addison smelt the alien male scent

gehorsam • lösten sich … von

an … gedrückt • Sirenengeheul • musste … widerstehen • überwältigend • Drang • und schritt über

Grundstück • fröstelte

wenig Aussicht haben … auf • Sieg • Wettbewerb • Schlimmeres

einvernehmliches Gemurmel • platschen • brüchig • Unglaube • Blitz • zerteilen • Donner • dumpfer Schlag • Beruhigung • näherte sich • vor Wut kochend • ragte über • fremdartig

of pipe tobacco and Brylcreem and malt whisky. Addison was terrified, but he had heard that one word – *son*. This must be the moment (quite different from the one in his imagination) when his father was going to claim him as his own. Addison stood up straight and tried to look Bill Addison in the eye, an impossibility given the way his father was towering over him. Addison tried to think of the right thing to say but only one word came to his mind. 'Father,' he said, hearing how tinny and useless his voice sounded. Before he had a chance to compose anything else Bill Addison unleashed a blow like a thunderbolt (for a moment Addison wondered if he had actually been struck by lightning) and he found himself sprawled, full-length, on the lawn.

All Addison could see was a great bowl of purple, rain-darkened sky above his head. He could hear his mother spitting out obscenities. His father roared, 'Whore!' at her in an enraged, apoplectic tone and one of the women screamed in horror at the word, although not nearly as much as when his mother yelled back at his father that he was 'a fucking, cunting whoremaister'. The words sounded fuzzy to Addison, it was only later in the hospital that he discovered his eardrum had burst. Blood ran down his face from his nose and dripped onto the grass and when he tried to turn his head a spasm of hot pain shot through it. Tears started to roll down his face and mingled with the blood. The lawn, he noticed, was not as green close up as it had looked from a distance.

Then his mother screamed, 'Fucking rapist!' and Bill Addison began to hit Shirley. Addison heard someone say, 'Hang on there, Bill,' and get thumped for their trouble. A bolt of lightning rent a fissure across the sky. A thunderclap exploded above his head and Addison decided he was dead.

He was brought to life again by a deluge of rain. The smell of wet earth and grass was oddly comforting,

Pfeife • (Pomade) • Malz
ragte über … empor
zu erdichten • rausließ • Hieb • Donnerschlag • vom Blitz getroffen • ausgestreckt • in voller Länge • Schale • Obszönitäten • Hure • aufgebracht • kurz vorm Schlaganfall • Scheiß- • Hurenbock • undeutlich • Trommelfell • geplatzt war • Krampf • vermischten sich mit • aus der Nähe • Vergewaltiger • wurde geschlagen • Mühe • riss • Spalt • Donnerschlag • Guss

although for the rest of his life a sudden summer downpour would make Addison's heart contract with an unnameable grief.
A pair of small feet appeared by his head. The feet were encased in frilled white socks and white Clark's sandals. Addison had never seen socks that white. The owner of the feet dropped to their knees by his side. Addison found himself looking up into Susan's solemn face. Her hair had been turned to wet strings by the rain and her pink dress now clung damply to her body. Silently, she placed the toy aeroplane on the grass next to him. Addison licked his dry lips and tried to form a word of thanks but then Susan was dragged away by her mother.

Platzregen • unsagbar
ummantelt • gerüscht • (Markenname) • ernst • Strähnen • feucht
leckte

*

Addison had just arrived at an accident on the M9 when Clare went into premature labour. It was raining and they'd had a call on the radio to say 'the VA looks as if it's going to prove' (the 'fatal' was always left off the end of this sentence – Addison sometimes wondered if it was out of a kind of delicacy). By the time they had got there it was all over and there was

frühzeitige Wehen bekam • (= victim of accident) Unfallopfer • tödlich • Feingefühl

Ergänzen Sie das zugehörige Substantiv/Adjektiv: **Übung 15**

Substantiv	Adjektiv
impossibility	________
________	troublesome
solemnity	________
________	fatal
________	imaginative
________	delicate
apoplexy	________
________	damp
________	obscene

nothing to do but stand around helplessly looking at the smashed-up Audi A4 and somebody's wife, somebody's mother lying all broken up on the road. Addison wished his own wife wouldn't drive so fast. That was when Robbie got the call to say that Clare had been taken into hospital and Addison thought there was something weird about that – the one life just ended, the other about to begin. What if the soul of this dead woman had flown into the body of his own child? They didn't know if it was a boy or a girl because Clare wanted to be surprised. Addison wasn't so keen on surprises himself. He hoped it was a girl. Clare laughed and said she just hoped it was a baby.

It turned out that the one thing that Clare didn't do quickly was give birth. There were 'complications' but no one made it very clear what they were and Addison was left stranded in a small waiting room on his own. Addison was used to being in charge at accidents (this felt like an accident) and didn't know what to do with this powerlessness. He stared at the floor in front of his feet and found himself wondering if it was going to prove.

They nearly lost the baby, then they nearly lost Clare. Was that what she had been doing – racing against

demoliert

komisch

in ... geflogen war • war nicht so scharf auf

wurde ... seinem Schicksal überlassen • allein • die Verantwortung zu tragen • Machtlosigkeit • um die Wette laufen mit ...

Übung 16 Vervollständigen Sie die Sätze, indem Sie die inhaltlich richtige Aussage ankreuzen.

1. While the baby was being born,

☐ a woman died in a car crash.

☐ Addison got a speeding ticket.

☐ Addison got a phone call from his father.

2. In the hospital Addison waited

☐ in the cafeteria.

☐ in a crowded waiting room.

☐ alone in a small waiting room.

life, trying to keep one step ahead of the open grave? Eventually, Addison was taken to see her. She looked a strange green colour but she was all right. She smiled at him as if it was her role to cheer him up. Addison couldn't think of anything to say so he just sat by the bed holding her hand and must have fallen asleep because a nurse was shaking him gently awake and asking him if he'd like to see his son. For a minute Addison had no idea what she was talking about.

Despite the tubes and dials that adorned his ICU cot, the baby looked healthier than his mother. The nurse told Addison that he was going to pull through, in a way that seemed absurdly confident to Addison. Clare didn't seem so convinced either when he went back to her single-bedded room. Addison knew it wasn't a good sign that she was in a room on her own. He wondered if it would be better if he was more optimistic or would that be like asking for trouble?

Clare wanted to give the baby a name straight away but as neither of them wanted religion involved she suggested they put an announcement in the paper. Clare insisted that Addison decide on a name – they had already drawn up a shortlist of five – and Addison

einen Schritt voraus zu sein • Grab • ihn aufzumuntern • hatte keine Ahnung • Schläuche • Anzeigen • verzierten • (= intensive care unit) Intensivstation • Kinderbett • durchkommen würde • Einzelzimmer • Ärger heraufzubeschwören • sofort • Anzeige • eine Liste der engeren Auswahl … angefertigt

3. The new-born child

- had some health problems and was unlikely to survive.
- looked healthier than his mother.
- was quite heavy.

4. Addison and Clare

- already had a name for their new-born child.
- had five possible names for the baby.
- had no idea what name to call the baby.

finally settled on Ewan because it seemed Scottish but not too Scottish. The outside world – wet and cold – hit Addison like a blow when he left the overheated bubble of the hospital. He really didn't know if he could take the lifetime of worry that lay ahead of him now that he had a child.

The next day Addison bought a copy of the *Evening News* to check the announcement was in. It was and it looked solid and certain. The baby existed, it had a name, a name in print. Addison had never in his life read the Births and Deaths column but now it took on a personal interest and he glanced idly through the list of names, vaguely curious about the children who shared a birth date with his own son – a Connor and an Amelia. His eye was caught by the first announcement in the Deaths column – 'Addison'. For a paranoid moment Addison thought it was some kind of foretelling of his own death and then he realized it was his father. His father was dead.

entschied sich … für • traf … wie ein Schlag • Blase • die lebenslängliche Sorge • (Abendzeitung) beständig • abgedruckt • Spalte mit den Geburts- und Todesanzeigen • in aller Ruhe • vage • neugierig • Voraussage

The funeral was in the crematorium. Addison sat in the back row, near the door. Marjorie Addison, now a bent and shrivelled figure, was seated at the front, nearest to the coffin. She had had to be supported into

Begräbnisfeier • gebeugt • verschrumpelt • Sarg

Übung 17 In allen gesuchten Wörtern steckt der Buchstabe „u". Finden Sie die englischen Begriffe anhand der Umschreibungen.

1. wanting to know everything _ u _ _ _ u _
2. chewing gum can be blown into a _ u _ _ _ _
3. burial or cremation of a dead person _ u _ _ _ _ _
4. having a big belly _ _ u _ _ _ _
5. a person who feels grief or sorrow _ _ u _ _ _ _
6. not well-dressed _ _ u _ _ _
7. not clearly or distinctly _ _ _ u _ _ _

the crematorium by her two sons, Douglas and Andrew, one on either side of her, but now that she was seated it was her daughters who sat with her. Pam, frumpy in washed-out black, dabbed her eyes from time to time. Next to her Susan remained dry-eyed throughout, staring at the coffin with a kind of defiance.

Thanks to a short obituary piece in the *Evening News*, Addison knew that his father had handed on the garage empire to Douglas and Andrew ten years ago but right up to the end had interfered in the running of it ('never quite let go of the reins'). Addison's brothers sat with their heads bowed, unwaveringly solemn expressions fixed on their faces. Halfway through the service, Douglas glanced at his watch. They were both big, built like rugby players, but close up he could see they looked too paunchy to be really fit. Addison reckoned he could take both of them if he had to – not that he was planning to, but the last time he had made a claim to his birthright ('Father–') it had ended in violence and there was no guarantee it wouldn't go the same way this time.

The service was a perfunctory sort of affair, lacking in emotion and built out of clichés – 'pillar of the business community', 'stalwart of the Rotary Club', 'an Olympian'. Addison hoped that he wouldn't have a funeral service. Perhaps he could persuade Clare to take his body to some clifftop somewhere and build him a funeral pyre and set it alight in one last blaze of glory so that he could rise up into the atmosphere and circle the earth as dust and ashes. His father's body, on the other hand, encased in polyester satin and ash veneer, disappeared discreetly behind a blue velvet curtain to be incinerated out of sight.

As the mourners filed out, the minister took up a position by the door, like a good maître d', and Addison had to suppress an urge to tip him.

ohne Schick • tupfte sich … ab • ungerührt • Trotz • Nachruf

hatte sich in … eingemischt • die Zügel losgelassen • unerschütterlich • dickbäuchig • Geburtsrecht • Gewalttätigkeit • oberflächlich • dem es an … fehlte • Säule • getreuer Anhänger • Trauergottesdienst • Klippenrand • Scheiterhaufen • in Glanz und Gloria • Eschenholz • Furnier • Samt • eingeäschert • Trauernde • nacheinander hinausgingen • Oberkellner • Trinkgeld zu geben

Addison followed the family back to the house. He found it hard to believe how much smaller it was than the baronial construct of his memory – no more than a detached Edinburgh villa with a few architectural curlicues.

konnte kaum glauben • feudal • frei stehend • Schnörkeln

As Addison started walking up the path his heart began to beat very fast and he found himself sweating inside his overcoat. He was gripped by an irrational fear that if he stepped over the threshold of his father's house he would be struck dead and it was only an act of sheer willpower that got him up the steps and through the glass doors of the porch.

Türschwelle

bloß • Willenskraft

The mourners were congregated in a large drawing room at the back of the house where a mock-Tudor bay looked out onto the garden, on which a winter gloom had already descended even though it was still early afternoon. The funeral tea was catered and the waiting staff moved quietly around the room, their expressions respectfully neutral. The atmosphere was that of a muted cocktail party.

waren versammelt • Salon • pseudo-Tudor (Baustil) • Erker • Düsterheit • Servierpersonal

gedämpft

Addison found himself standing near Pamela, Douglas and Andrew. Douglas and Andrew looked relieved, as if they couldn't wait to get on with their lives now.

erleichtert

'I never thought of him as someone who would die,' Pamela said.

'Well, it turns out that the old man was mortal like the rest of us,' Douglas said.

'You're so hard.'

'You should be harder.'

Douglas lit a cigarette and said, 'I thought he would never go.'

Andrew raised his glass to his brother in an ironic toast and murmured, 'The king is dead, long live the king.' Addison imagined the shock on their faces if he suddenly declared himself as one of them. But it was too late, and somehow it didn't mean anything any more. There was nothing left to do but leave.

Susan was standing at the open front door, holding a

bottle of malt. She was looking at the rain but when she saw Addison she smiled as if she'd been expecting him and offered him the malt. Addison shook his head, even though the whisky looked like the best thing he'd seen all day. Addison had been a teetotaller since attending his first fatal VA six years ago – three children from the back seat of a Nissan scattered all over the M90 thanks to a whisky-sodden accountant in a Mercedes. One of the children was still alive when Addison peeled her off the tarmac. Would Clare agree never to take their own child out in the car? Hardly likely.

He knew Susan had three children of her own. She was a lawyer. He knew this from an article she'd written in the *Scotsman* about domestic abuse and the law. There had been a photograph of her in which she looked more carefree than she did now.

'Are they all going on about how wonderful he was?' Susan asked. Addison was unnerved by the way she spoke to him as if she'd known him all her life. She didn't seem to expect an answer so Addison didn't give one. She tucked her hair behind her ears, a gesture that made her seem touchingly young.

'I hated him,' she said simply.

Antialkoholiker • über … verstreut • Whisky-trunkenen • vom … abzog • Asphalt • (Zeitung) • Gewalt in der Familie • sorglos • aus der Fassung gebracht • streifte • Geste • rührend

Übung 18

Ergänzen Sie die fehlenden Vergangenheitsformen der unregelmäßigen Verben:

to find	________	found
to think	thought	________
to mean	________	meant
to know	________	known
to do	did	________
to speak	________	spoken
to make	made	________
to have	had	________

'Oh?' Addison said.

'He was a bully and a drinker. And a philanderer. I think he abused my sister, but she won't talk about it. He had no idea how to love. Love's the most important thing, you know.'

'That's what they say.'

'You think it's a sentimental cliché.'

'No. No, I don't,' Addison said. He thought about telling her that his wife had just had a baby, that they were both still in the hospital in a state of disrepair, but the whole idea of fatherhood was still so raw and unformed that he knew he would start crying if he talked about it.

Susan was holding herself as if she was very cold and suddenly every nerve and fibre and cell in Addison's body yearned to declare itself kin. Instead he said, 'Well, he's gone now,' but it came out sounding more harsh than he'd intended.

'He'll never go,' Susan said blankly. 'He'll never die. We'll carry him around inside ourselves for ever. You can't imagine what it was like to be his child.'

'No,' Addison agreed, 'I can't. I have to go,' he added awkwardly.

'Of course.'

Tyrann • Schürzenjäger • missbrauchte

in einem schlechten Zustand • Vaterschaft

Faser • verlangte danach • verwandt • barsch

linkisch

Übung 19 Welche Satzteile gehören zusammen? Tragen Sie die entsprechenden Buchstaben in die Kästchen ein.

1. Susan believed that her father had abused her sister,
2. Addison thought about telling her
3. The idea of being a father was still so new
4. When Addison declared that his father was dead
5. Addison was surprised by his own gesture,

Addison bent down and kissed Susan on the cheek. He was more surprised by this gesture than she was and, feeling oddly embarrassed, he turned up his collar against the rain and walked swiftly out of the door. The segs on his shoes struck off the York-stone slabs of the path, an echo of something he couldn't quite remember.

verlegen • eilig • Schuhbeschläge

When he got to the gate, he looked back. Susan was still standing there, watching him.

a) that he might start crying if he talked about it.

b) but she wouldn't talk about it.

c) actually a lot more than Susan was.

d) it came out a lot harsher than originally intended.

e) that his wife had just had a baby.

Beareth all things,
believeth all things,
hopeth all things,
endureth all things.

ST PAUL, I CORINTHIANS, 13:7

For Maureen Allan

Dissonance

Simon wished his mother would die. Right that minute. Right where she was sitting, which was almost undoubtedly down in the kitchen, at the bloody kitchen table, doing her bloody marking. *I'm at my wits' end with you, Simon. I worry about what's going to happen to you, I really do.* Well, if she was dead she wouldn't have to worry, would she? And he wouldn't have to listen to her bloody nagging. *Shoes don't live in the kitchen, Simon. If you spill something, do you think you could wipe it up, Simon? Do you know what a dishwasher's for, Simon?* He knew what would go on her bloody headstone as well. *I've just cleaned that, Simon.*

Korn's *Life is Peachy* pounded on the stereo, helping keep his thoughts in rhythm with Tekken 3 on the PlayStation. Hwoarang hammered machine-gun punches into Lei Wulong's stomach *Simon, if you're going to finish all the milk, could you buy more?* Paul Phoenix pulled a three-hit combo with a God Hammer punch on Yoshimitsu *If you use something, could you put it back when you've finished with it, Simon?* Simon snorted with adolescent schadenfreude as he imagined his mother in the King of the Iron Fists tournament, Forest Law thwacking junkyard kicks into her virtual body parts, Jin Kazama chopping her into submission *Do you remember when you used to kiss and cuddle me and call me 'Mummy'?*

She was going to tell his father. *Shoplifting, Simon. That's theft, pure and simple.* Like the shops weren't ripping him off in the first place. *And how do you work that one out, Simon?* She knew he couldn't argue like Rebecca. She was always trying to get him

gleich

Korrigieren

Nörgelei • Grabstein • (sogen. Nu Metal Band) • (Titel der CD) • (Name des Spiels) • Kombination aus drei Schlägen • prustete ... vor • Wettkampf • schlug • (Bezeichnung für spezielle Tritte in Tekken) • hackte • Unterwerfung • gekuschelt • Ladendiebstahl • nicht ... ausnahmen • von vornherein • und wie bist du zu diesem Schluss gekommen

to explain things. *Why did you do that, Simon? What were you thinking?* Stupid cow. *Just because your father doesn't live with us any more doesn't mean he can* ***abdicate his responsibilities****.* 'Tell Dad if you want, I haven't even seen him **in weeks**.' Dad wasn't interested in them any more anyway. He had Jenny now. *It'll never last.* Jenny who was pregnant, **except** their mother didn't know it. *What do you think will happen to you if you keep on this path, Simon? Hm?* King punched Ling Xiaoyu and then jumped on her body. KO. Ling Xiaoyu gave a girly little scream. Game Over. You Win.

sich der Verantwortung entziehen • seit Wochen • nur dass

Rebecca was making a **bar chart** for Higher Maths to the **untroubling** sound of **Travis** on her **headphones**. She was using Excel – **neat** blocks of red, blue, green and purple that would come out nicely on her Epson colour printer. Rebecca liked everything to be neat. Her room was completely coordinated – lilacs, purples and blues, a touch of pink but not too girly. She didn't think of herself as a girly girl. The cover on her bed was pulled **smooth**, her books and **files aligned with** the **edge** of her **shelf**. *You* ***take after*** *your father, don't you?*

Säulendiagramm • nicht störend • (schottische Rockband) • Kopfhörer • ordentlich • glatt • Aktenordner • bündig ausgerichtet an • Kante • Regal • gerätst nach

Übung 20 In dem Buchstabendickicht sind neun englische Begriffe versteckt. Angeordnet sind sie waagerecht (von links nach rechts), senkrecht (von oben nach unten) und diagonal (von links oben nach rechts unten).

Die deutschen Übersetzungen der Wörter lauten: glatt, sich entziehen, ordentlich, nur dass, Kopfhörer, schuldig, bündig ausrichten, Teekessel, überfallen.

Suchen und markieren Sie die Begriffe.

She checked the clock. 21.43. At ten o'clock she'd make hot chocolate. Rebecca thought she might buy a kettle and a small microwave for her bedroom. She had enough money, she'd worked as soon as she could get a job – down at the Alldays, in the video shop – now she worked in Superdrug on Saturdays and holidays. Her own money, not guilty paternal handouts. *You're so selfsufficient, Rebecca.* If she had a microwave and a kettle she'd never have to bother with the rest of the house, apart from the bathroom. It was a shame her Superdrug job didn't run to funding an en-suite bathroom, then she could just stay in her own neat nest. She couldn't wait to be living in a hall of residence.
22.00. Rebecca removed her headphones and was assaulted by the noise from Simon's stereo. No wonder he had mince for brains. And he played such shite. Korn, for Christ's sake. *I don't know, when I was your age songs used to have a tune.* When their mother came out with her nostalgia crap Rebecca felt the same irritation as her brother but she would never give him the pleasure of sibling camaraderie by telling him that. Their mother talked about her youth a lot these days, ever since Beardy Brian came on the scene. They used

Teekessel

(Supermarktkette) • (Drogeriekette) • schuldbewusst • selbstständig • nicht ausreichte um …

Studentenwohnheim • wurde von … überfallen • Hackfleisch • Herrgott noch mal

n	o	m	s	m	o	o	t	h	i	r	t
m	h	i	p	c	l	r	t	o	o	h	a
e	h	e	v	k	a	n	e	a	t	s	b
x	m	o	a	r	e	z	h	t	u	g	d
c	p	e	t	d	i	t	s	c	m	y	i
e	x	i	y	n	p	v	t	k	u	o	c
p	w	z	b	c	u	h	i	l	q	j	a
t	s	l	e	f	m	g	o	a	e	w	t
o	e	p	q	j	r	e	n	n	v	x	e
c	g	u	i	l	t	y	t	q	e	r	m
x	t	a	s	s	a	u	l	t	l	s	o
a	n	t	o	g	a	l	i	g	n	e	k

to be at university together, a fact that seemed to continually amaze them both – *Who'd have thought then that we'd get together?* – as if they were the only two Aberdeen university alumni on the planet.

'Alumni'. That was a word she had learnt from Beardy Brian. She'd tucked it away for further use. 'Yes, I'm a Trinity alumnus.' They did Latin at Watson's, she knew her plurals. Their mother never stopped telling them how lucky they were to do Latin. *In my day everyone did it. Now you only get taught it if you go to expensive schools like yours. What about my poor kids, don't they deserve the choice?* But they had never had Latin on the curriculum at the schemie school her mother taught at and she knew it.

Not that Rebecca was sure about Cambridge. There were plenty of places she could apply to. *But Edinburgh has an excellent reputation for medicine – then you could live at home.* Yeah, that'll be right.

Not that she was entirely sure about medicine either. Her subjects were strong across the board, maybe she should do an Arts degree. But when she thought of herself in the future – which was all the time – she saw herself as a doctor, not in some scummy NHS* hospital but as a surgeon with Médecins sans Fron-

zu erstaunen … schien • ehemalige Studenten • verstaute • weitere Verwendung • (Singular von alumni) • (abkürzend für dortige Eliteuniversität) • Ruf • völlig • Unterrichtsfächer • gut • durch die Bank • Geisteswissenschaften • schmierig • Chirurgin

info

NHS ist die Abkürzung für **National Health Service** und bezeichnet das staatliche Gesundheitssystem in Großbritannien, das seit 1948 existiert. Es garantiert jeder in GB wohnhaften Person medizinische Versorgung.

Médecins sans Frontières (dt.: Ärzte ohne Grenzen) ist eine 1971 gegründete internationale und unabhängige Hilfsorganisation, die in Krisen- und Kriegsgebieten medizinische Nothilfe leistet.

„The Female Eunuch“ (dt.: „Der weibliche Eunuch“), geschrieben von Germaine Greer, erschien 1970 und wurde ein internationaler Bestseller. Das kontrovers diskutierte Buch spielte für den Feminismus eine wichtige Rolle.

tières*, operating in impossible conditions in a war zone, or a doctor in some remote mountain village vaccinating the photogenic babies of noble tribeswomen. Dr Rebecca McFarlane.

Rebecca opened Simon's door and yelled at him to turn his stereo down. His face flushed a furious fuchsia at this intrusion.

'You wouldn't stand for it if I came into your room without knocking, would you?'

'No, I'd fucking kill you,' she said matter-of-factly. It was hard to believe anyone she shared so many genes with could be so unattractive. Simon had spots like Braille. A blind person could probably read half of Shakespeare on his face. 'It stinks in here, Simon.'

'Leave then.'

'No, really. I'm serious, it's disgusting.'

You do shower every day, don't you, Simon?

'I said leave.'

'You shouldn't wank so much in here.'

She managed to close the door just in time for his trainer to thud off it. 'Whore,' he yelled as Rebecca ran lightly down the stairs, laughing.

Their mother was standing at the kitchen door, a frown contracting her round moon features, her voice full of concern. *Did he just call you a whore, Becca?* 'Yeah, you'd better go and throw *The Female Eunuch** at him.' *You can't call women whores, even if you don't mean it.* 'But what about if they actually are whores?' *It's a derogatory term. Language is how we define our world.* 'Yeah, use that argument on Simon, why don't you, like he'll really understand what you're talking about.'

Her mother was wearing that disgusting, worn-out denim smock that looked as if she'd had it since she was pregnant. She looked pregnant in it now. She had no waistline whatsoever. She took her glasses off and let them dangle on the chain which bounced off her cushiony breasts as she walked up the stairs. She might as well not be wearing a bra.

die … impft • Stammesfrauen

errötete • Einmischung •

würdest es auch nicht hinnehmen • sachlich

Pickel • Blindenschrift

solltest … nicht … wichsen •

Turnschuh • abprallte

Sorge

abfälliger Ausdruck

Hängekleid aus Jeans • Taille • überhaupt keine • baumeln • von … abprallte • kissenweich • BH

Her mother's underwear was horrible, everything slightly grey and stretched, the elastic gone in the M and S sports bras she wore, even though she was the least sporty person Rebecca could think of. Rebecca did her own washing. The idea of contaminating anything she wore with her mother's saggy bras and washed-to-death Sloggis or – infinitely worse – Simon's skid-marked, urine-spotted boxers, *At least make an effort to aim for the toilet bowl, Simon*, made her feel ill.

Rebecca's underwear was spotlessly white – she presoaked it in Vanish – she preferred white and so, luckily, did her boyfriend, Fraser. Fraser was as good as they got, captain of the rugby team and Dux of the school, he had his own car and was allowed to have Rebecca to stay whenever he wanted, although they never had sex in his house, Rebecca couldn't bear the idea of Fraser's mother listening to them. Rebecca was going to finish with Fraser when she went to university. It was a curiously empty relationship, not based on passion, something Rebecca was looking forward to experiencing one day.

Her mother had been listening to Classic FM – a Mahler symphony, Rebecca didn't know which one. She didn't like Mahler. Rebecca whisked the hot chocolate into a pan of milk. Her mother had a still-warm cup of camomile tea next to her pile of marking. *'Update* Romeo and Juliet *to the modern-day world'.* Oh for Christ's sake, they'd just write about the Baz Luhrmann film. Or Northern Ireland, or Bosnia, except they wouldn't know where that was. How clichéd. Why couldn't they just study the bloody text? *You have to make literature relevant to real life.* Why? Rebecca leafed idly through the top essay, a scrawled, messy affair. She smirked at the conclusion, 'What a sheer, big waste of love *Romeo and Juliet* is!' What a moron. She could hear her mother's one-sided conversation with Simon, her mother on her side of the door remonstrating with that reasonable whine in her

unsportlichste
• verunreinigen
• ausgeleiert •
unendlich •
mit „Bremsspu-
ren“

weichte …
vorab ein •
(Fleckenentfer-
ner, wörtl.: Ver-
schwinde) •
besser als mit
… wurde es
nicht •
Schulbester •
seltsam

verquirlte •
Milchtopf •
Kamillentee

blätterte durch
• gekritzelt •
unordentlich •
grinste … über
• Schlussfolge-
rung • Ver-
schwendung •
Schwachkopf •
protestierend •
vernunftbetont
• Winseln

voice, Simon on the other side grunting like pre-literate Cro-Magnon man. In fact, if you thought of Simon as an unsuccessful example of Early Man his entire existence was easier to make sense of.

Her mother plodded back down the stairs. Rebecca could only see her legs through the banisters – white and veined, and her ankles like melting Brie above those bloody awful faux-Birkenstocks. She sighed as she came into the kitchen. Her mother had a huge lexicon of sighs. A sigh for every occasion. Her Simon sigh was always a particularly heavy one.

He's got Standard Grades next year, she said, as if Rebecca might be interested, as if Rebecca was the other parent for God's sake.

'Like I care.'

You didn't think to ask if I wanted any hot chocolate then? her mother said, adding a *no one in this house ever thinks about me* sigh.

'You've got camomile tea.' *The only conversations we ever have are arguments, have you ever thought about that, Rebecca?* 'Well, maybe that's your fault, have you ever thought about that, "Mother"?'

Rebecca left the kitchen abruptly. She wasn't going to give her mother the satisfaction of any kind of conver-

grunzte • vor der Entwicklung einer geschriebenen Sprache existierend • trottete … wieder hinunter • Treppengeländer • adrig • Knöchel • unecht • (Prüfung am Ende der elften Klasse)

Auseinandersetzungen

Genugtuung

Übung 21

Ordnen Sie die folgenden Wörter aus dem Text einem bedeutungsähnlichen Begriff in der rechten Spalte zu.

curiously	flabby
leaf through	untidy
saggy	failing
grunt	strangely
fault	grumble
messy	browse

knallte … zu • Hirnblutung

sation. She slammed her bedroom door. 'Why don't you just die,' she muttered. 'Drop dead of a brain haemorrhage and leave us to get on with our lives.'

(US-amerikanische Metal-Band) • (Name einer fiktiven Band) • sich die Mühe zu machen, sich • (Figur aus Tekken 3) • (US-amerikanische Nu-Metal-band) • Schrott • (Klavierwerk von Johann Sebastian Bach)

Simon turned his stereo up. Machine Head, *The Burning Red*. Boak's first album, *Guts for Garters*. He got into bed without bothering to undress and fell asleep imagining he was Eddie Gordo kicking and spinning and punching to his own beat. One day everyone would know the name of Simon McFarlane. Know it and fear it.

Slipknot, for God's sake. Surely their mother wasn't going to let him play that junk so loud at this time of night? What did the neighbours think? (God, had she really just thought that?) She put her headphones on and fell asleep listening to the 'Goldberg' Variations.

*

A nice family dinner. Nothing special.
But Beardy Brian wasn't family. He was a bloody stranger. A bloody stranger who was doing it with

Übung 22 Kreuzen Sie das richtige Satzende an.

1. Rebecca wished her mother would die of a

tumor. brain haemorrhage. heart attack.

2. Simon went to bed without bothering to

pray. wash. undress.

3. Rebecca fell asleep listening to

Bach. Slipknot. Mozart.

their mother – no, don't let your thoughts even go there, Simon.

Try and sit up straight, Simon. You'll give yourself back problems when you're older. 'I'm not going to be older.' *Don't be silly.*

Silly? That was her, with her manners and her rules and conscience. *Privileges come with duties attached.* What the fuck did that mean? Silly was what Beardy Brian made her. She had new clothes on – some kind of weird ethnic shite, and make-up which she only usually put on for parents' evenings – theirs and hers. And he knew for a fact that she had new underwear because he'd seen La Senza carrier bags all over the place. Don't go there, Simon.

Beardy Brian was so boring. He was some kind of social worker, so that suited his mother down to the ground. He was gulping the good red that she'd bought two bottles of from Oddbins, instead of her usual cheap stuff from Somerfield, for the *family dinner* and talking earnestly at her. 'They've ring-fenced the funding for youth work but that's not good enough you need a much bigger investment blah blah blah.' She loved all that stuff. *Oh, it's not even a case of investment – although it is, of course – it's more to do*

Rückenschmerzen • albern • Umgangsformen • Gewissen • verbunden • (Dessous-Ladenkette) • Tragetaschen • überall • war ideal für • kippte ... hinunter • (Weinhandlungskette) • (Kette kleinerer Supermärkte) • an einen bestimmten Verwendungszweck gebunden

4. For Simon and Rebecca, Beardy Brian was
family. a stranger. a good friend.

5. Their mother used to say: "Privileges come with duties
aside." together." attached."

6. Beardy Brian earns his money as a
teacher. social worker. wine merchant.

wurden von … aufgegeben • verurteilen •	*with imagination, these kids have been abandoned by society and then people condemn them for asocial behaviour –*
absurd • Gähnen	'I know, I know, it's ridiculous, Pam.' And on and on. Big yawn. Pam and Brian. The perfect couple.
	'For God's sake, Simon,' his sister snarled, 'close your mouth when you eat. I really don't need to see the contents of your stomach.'
Erwachsene	His sister actually believed she was a grown-up. Rebecca was going to be just like their mother when she did grow up. Ha ha. That would be funny – the worst thing she could ever think of was going to hap-
würde ihr recht geschehen • Mühe geben	pen to her. That would serve her right. *They used to be so close when they were little.* Yeah, right, I don't think so. *Couldn't you just once make an effort?* At least Beardy Brian for dinner meant that they were having a roast. Roast Pork. Sweet. They hadn't had that since their father left. Funny that. Rebecca had
Folie • furzen • kicherte	some piece of vegetarian crap in a foil container. 'You'll fart all night,' he snickered at her.
	Simon! 'What? It's a natural bodily function. We all fart. You fart all the time.' *Simon!*
	Beardy Brian looked embarrassed. 'She does,' Simon said. 'You'll find out. If you haven't already.'

Übung 23

Finden Sie die auf dieser Doppelseite vorkommenden englischen Begriffe anhand der Umschreibungen.

1. adult ________________

2. to laugh in a half-suppressed way ________________

3. as a last means, when everything else has failed ________________

4. beer brewed in a special way ________________

5. embarrassing ________________

6. absurd ________________

Simon. Enough!

Awkward silence, awkward for them anyway. Simon didn't feel awkward, he just wanted to get as much dead pig down his throat as fast as possible. 'Fatal wind.' Simon giggled. *I'm sorry?* 'Tekken,' Simon said. 'It's a character you can get called Panda. Panda's cool, he can crush you to death. Plus he farts. Fatal wind.' *He's a good boy really. He's just at that age.* She'd made pudding too. Tiramisu. Could almost be the name of a Tekken fighter. He heh, heh, heh. 'Won't you share the joke, Simon?' Beardy Brian, being all chummy. *Boys have it very difficult these days, Brian.* 'Tell me about it, Pam. Sometimes you wonder if they didn't have it right in the old days, channel all that testosterone, Spartan youth, Achilles, Herakles … warriors.' Warriors, my arse, what did Beardy Brian know about warriors? Simon was a warrior, oh yes. *Oh, I don't know about that, Brian, there's never anything good about fighting.* 'No such thing as a just war, Pam?' *Yes, but violence is a* final *resort, Brian, surely?*

He was divorced but he didn't have any kids. *You haven't missed anything, Brian.* Did they really do it together? Beardy Brian with his beer belly – oh, sorry, 'real ale' belly – it couldn't be the same as sex between attractive people, it must be a completely different activity. Shagging his mother– Stop! Don't go there! No, but, really, it couldn't be like shagging Buffy, not that Simon wanted to shag Buffy (putting aside the fact she'd beat the crap out of him), she was too – what? Noble. Special. And heroic and vulnerable. You'd shag Romney Wright, you'd shag the women in porn mags, you wouldn't shag Buffy, you'd *court* her. Simon felt very pleased with that word. Court.

Simon, you've got gravy all down your chin.

Rebecca yelped with laughter. What a wanker. Simon had several astonishing new spots that had erupted on his forehead like plague pustules. He was like some

unangenehm

erdrücken

kumpelhaft

auf etwas richten • Krieger • dass ich nicht lache

Ausweg

(bestimmte Art der Bierverarbeitung und -darreichung) • zu bumsen • (weibl. Hauptfigur einer US-Fernseh-Serie) • verletzlich • Pornohefte • Soße • kreischte • erstaunlich • waren auf … ausgebrochen • Stirn • Pestbeulen

kind of bio-hazard. Pus at one end, methane at the other. *Exclusion's all very well, but how do you get them back into education?* Jesus, was it possible to have a more boring conversation? They were having sex, she knew that, it was an appalling thought but there was no doubt about it. She had heard them – eugh – they were trying to be quiet but her mother's bed was right next to the wall on the other side of Rebecca's so she couldn't help but hear the snuffling and shuffling and shushing, her mother's suppressed giggles, *Oh, God, don't look – keep the light off!* And the occasional tenor cry from him that sounded like pain. How could they sully her sleep like that? Even with the headphones on, even with Haydn's Second Cello Concerto, Coldplay, Spiritualized, Mozart's Flute Concerto in A – dear God, she'd tried everything – nothing muffled the fact that her mother was having it off with Beardy Brian less than a metre away from her head. How gross was that? Not even Slipknot could have exorcised that fact.

And had she thought of the consequences? Like, was she through the menopause? She looked like she was but maybe she wasn't. What if their mother got pregnant? Could Rebecca think of anything worse? Apart from failing her Highers, which was obviously not going to happen.

But perhaps Beardy Brian was better than Hawk. Hawk (like he'd been christened that, yeah, right), that lunatic aberration of last year after their father left. Hawk, the guy she had hired to do all those little odd jobs that somehow in her mind had been the responsibility of their father, which was a ridiculous flaw in her memory as their father, an advocate in the High Court, had never lifted a screwdriver in his life. Hawk was one of those loser hippy guys, all smug, cool, Zen philosophy and lazy smiles. You could tell he thought he was feline and irresistible but he must have been, God, at least thirty-five. He was the kind of

Eiter • entsetzlich • igitt • Schnaufen • Wälzen • Pst!-Sagen • unterdrückt • gelegentlich • besudeln • (brit. Pop-Rock-Band) • (brit. Rockband) • dämpfte • es mit … trieb • abstoßend • nicht bestehen • (schottische Hochschulreife) • getauft • irr • Fehltritt • Fehler • Rechtsanwalt • oberstes Gericht • Schraubenzieher • selbstgefällig • katzenartig • unwiderstehlich

guy who did it anywhere with anyone. Even their mother. He'd even tried it on with Rebecca one time when he was fixing a leaking tap in the bathroom, which, by the way, had leaked twice as much after he'd finished with it. He hadn't touched her or anything, he'd just said, Do you want to?, just like that. As if.
She'd heard them in *the reading group*, talking about him, her mother laughing, *it must be because he's got a toolbox*, and them all creasing themselves as if it was some kind of fantastic joke and one of them saying, 'Go, girlfriend,' like they were *black* or something when they were all just Corstorphine teacher-types. Once a month a *pot-luck supper* on a *revolving rota* at each other's houses. All they did was eat and drink (like fish) and gossip and poke into each other's bathrooms and wardrobes and lifestyles. They gave the book about ten minutes – *Captain Corelli*, The God of Small Things*, White Teeth** – nothing that wasn't popular and safe and digested by someone else first. Like Beardy Brian.
Aren't you going to have some tiramisu, Becca?
'It's delicious,' Beardy Brian said, wiping his beard with a napkin. Oh, God, no, they had photographs out now. Photographs of themselves as students – Beardy

undicht • Wasserhahn • doppelt so viel

Werkzeugkasten • kugelten sich vor Lachen • (Vorort von Edinburgh) • Abendessen, zu dem jeder Gast eine Speise mitbringt • abwechselnd • Plan • tratschen • die Nase in … stecken • vorgekaut • Serviette

info

Captain Corelli's Mandolin ist ein Roman von Louis de Bernières, der 1994 veröffentlicht wurde. Er spielt im Zweiten Weltkrieg und erzählt von der Liebesgeschichte zwischen Pelagia und dem italienischen Hauptmann Antonio Corelli. The God of Small Things (1997) ist ein politischer Roman der indischen Autorin Arundhati Roy, der mit dem Booker Prize ausgezeichnet wurde. Er erzählt die Geschichte zweier Zwillinge, deren Leben sich durch „small things“ dramatisch ändert. Zadie Smiths Roman White Teeth (2000) dreht sich um die unterschiedlichen Leben zweier früherer Kriegskameraden im London der 1970er Jahre.

Brian, bearded and boring even then, her mother all long hair and indifferent features. *Oh, God, look at that cloak I'm wearing! A cloak, for heaven's sake!* Her mother's forearm touching Brian's shirtsleeve. What had Dad ever *seen* in her?

Umhang • Unterarm

'You were always the brainy one, Pam.'

gescheit •

Why, thank you, kind sir. Yuck. Still, perhaps Beardy Brian would cushion their mother from Dad's news. If anyone ever got round to telling her. Jenny was five months gone already. Jenny, attractive and smart and fifteen whole years younger than their mother. Rebecca quite liked Jenny.

igitt • abfedern • war … im sechsten Monat

Where are you going, Simon? 'Out.' *We haven't finished.* 'I have.' *I thought we agreed you were grounded.* 'You agreed.' *What are you going to be doing, Simon? Are you meeting Jake and Angus? Simon, can you hear me?* 'Oh, shut the fuck up, will you.'

Hausarrest hast

'Simon!' Beardy Brian rose half out of his chair to remonstrate.

'Don't you tell me what to do, you're not my dad.' *No and I don't see your father in this room, do you, Simon?* 'No, he's with his bloody girlfriend, probably looking at bloody Mothercare shite.'

(engl. Ladenkette für Umstandskleidung, Baby- und Kinderkleidung und -artikel)

Übung 24 Lösen Sie das Kreuzworträtsel mithilfe der folgenden Erklärungen:

Across

1. a rattling sound

2. thankful

3. written account of facts

Down

4. intelligent

5. to feel less confident

6. to shake from cold or fear

7. to keep away from

Rebecca would have hit him if he'd been close enough. She could see that he was near to tears, he couldn't stop his lip trembling and his spots looked as if they were going to explode.

zitterte

What are you talking about? Where are you going? Come back, Simon. Simon!

The clatter and rumble of Simon's skateboard faded down the street. 'Jenny's pregnant,' Rebecca said in a flat voice, avoiding eye contact, looking at the pepper grinder instead. She could feel her mother deflate. Beardy Brian was looking ill at ease. Rebecca couldn't imagine he would actually want to be part of this *family*.

Scheppern • Donnern • vermied • Pfeffermühle • zusammensinken • unbehaglich

Rebecca cleared away the dishes from the table. She hated the way her mother looked so pathetically grateful for this act.

dankbar

✶

You were very lucky. An unofficial warning and no record. We don't have to tell the school. 'First offence – what are they gonna do, *bang me up for life*?' *They probably only let you get away with it because your father was there. What's the point of being an*

Eintrag ins Strafregister • Straftat eines Ersttäters • mich einbuchten • lebenslänglich

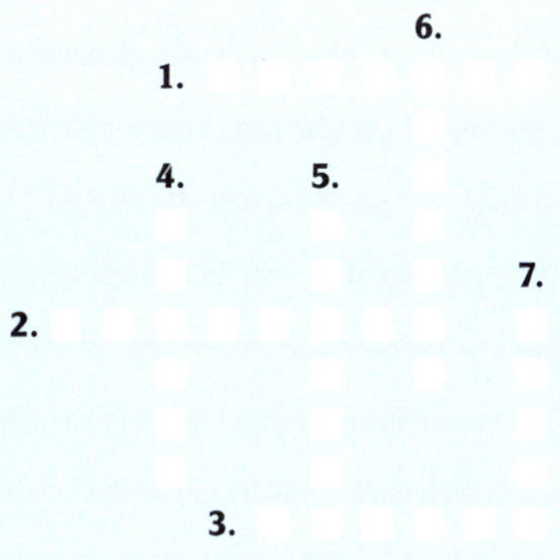

schade · großes Ehrenwort

advocate if you can't help your own child? 'Yeah, good old Dad. Shame you had to cry all over him. "Oh, Alistair, Alistair." Pathetic.' *Promise me you will never, ever–* 'Yeah, yeah, yeah, never do it again, cross my heart and hope to die blah blah blah. One fucking CD.'

Zeug

'How can she *believe* it was one CD?'
'Fuck off, Rebecca.'
'Fuck off yourself, Simon. You've stolen God knows how much stuff, your room's full of it – CDs, games, clothes – she thinks Dad's paying for it, it's not like he doesn't give you money, but I mean she must be stupid or really naive – which she is, we know–'
'Rebecca?'
'What?'
'Shut the fuck up, will you.'
'No, I won't, it's time somebody said something to you.'

stolzierst … herum • kicherten … über

'Oh and you're that person, are you? I don't think so. You think you're so bloody perfect. You and your friends. You swagger around school like you're so special.' Hannah, Sarah, Emma. God, how Simon hated them, always sniggering at him, laughing at every-

Übung 25 Welches Wort passt nicht zu den anderen in der Gruppe? Kreuzen Sie es an.

1. pitiful · pathetic · moving · illicit

2. to snigger · to snuffle · to giggle · to laugh

3. punch · kick · step · poke

thing he said, treating him like an idiot. 'A fine example of Early Man. Ha ha.'
'What have my friends got to do with anything?'
Hannah-Sarah-Emma – one entity in Simon's head. They were all going to be so sorry one day. He was going to punch them and kick them like Paul Phoenix kicking Ling Xiaoyu until they shut their mouths. That would surprise them. Or shag the lot of them – and they'd all think he was fantastic – Hannah-Sarah-Emma, all tossing their shiny hair and going down on him and moaning, a lot of moaning–
'Well? Can't you speak?'
'Shut up.'
'You're so articulate, Simon.'
'You're such a bitch.'
'You're such a wanker.'
'Cow.'
'Prick.'
'Whore.'
'Virgin.'
'Cunt.'
Simon? Simon? Did you just call your sister what I think you called her?
'Cunt, Mother,' Rebecca said sweetly, passing her mother on the stairs, 'he called me a cunt.'

Deftones. Tekken. A Pot Noodle. Another Pot Noodle. Half a sliced pan loaf with butter and jam. One illicit can of lager. Three illicit fags smoked out of the window. One last round of Tekken. Sleep. Dreams of world dominance and Hannah-Sarah-Emma giving him a blow job.

Mozart's *Requiem*. *Portrait of a Lady*. An apple. Half a bar of Dairy Milk. The cat purring on the bed. Hot chocolate and a small neatly rolled joint. Sleep. Dreams of the Chinese boy who sometimes delivered their takeaway and saving Simon from the Forth in

behandelten ihn wie
Einheit
(Figuren aus Tekken 3)
zurückwarfen • Stöhnen
redegewandt • Miststück
Schwanz
Fotze
(US-amerikanische Rockband) • (Nudel-Fertiggericht) • verboten • Dose • Lagerbier • Kippen • (Roman von Henry James, 1996 verfilmt) • Riegel • (beliebte Schokoladenmarke) • schnurrend • Essen zum Mitnehmen

flood. He was so dream-heavy that she thought she might have to let him slip back into the water. Then she woke up.

✶

Pfirsich • (britische Tageszeitung) • zuckte mit den Schultern

Rebecca ate a peach for breakfast. 'No Brian?' *No.* Her mother was sitting at the table reading the *Guardian* and eating muesli that looked like chicken feed. 'But it's Saturday morning.' *So?* Rebecca shrugged. Beardy Brian always stayed on a Friday night but she didn't really care enough to enter into a conversation about his absence. *It's a lovely day.* 'Mm.' Rebecca gave the cat a saucer of milk. *We could go to something in the Festival* this morning.* 'I'm going to something already.' Her mother looked at her over the top of her glasses, smiling, very teacher. *Oh, what?* All excited and interested. 'Mozart Quartets. Queen's Hall.' *Well, maybe I could come with you?* 'Sold out.' *Oh. Are you going with Fraser?* 'Fraser? No.'

Abwesenheit • Untertasse

Warteschlange • schlurften … hin und her • missmutig • Vorführung • „Mandel-Hockey" • hässlichsten • (brit. Heavy-Metal-Band) • Fettqualle • hübsch • Hüpfburg • Titten • „Schmuggel von Patronenkugeln"

Simon at the bus stop, head full of nothing, arms full of skateboard. There was a couple ahead of him in the queue who were trying to see how far down each other's throats they could get. Disgusting. The old people waiting for the 41 shuffled discontentedly at this display of tonsil hockey. Simon liked that phrase, tonsil hockey. It was stupid and it removed any potential for tenderness. They were two of the ugliest people he'd ever seen. They were both dressed in black. The guy was tall and hairy and young with an Iron Maiden T-shirt. The girl was huge. Fat. Simon just wanted to stare at her arse and thighs. What a bloater! And not bonny, oh no. It must be like shagging a bouncy castle. And her norks! Like a hundred times bigger than his sister's. Why was he thinking about his sister's norks? Gross. He could see the tonsil hockey girl's nipples through her black top. Smuggling bullets. Heh, heh, heh.

'Your type, is she?'

Fucking Rebecca. 'Fuck off.' The old people shuffled more agitatedly, one or two of them muttered about Simon's language, about Rebecca's queue jumping. The 41 sailed into view and Simon made a point of not letting the old people on first, mumbling 'Day Saver' at the bus driver and rushing up the stairs to get away from his sister.

aufgeregt • brummelten • Vordrängelei • Tageskarte

'Don't mind me sitting here, do you?' Rebecca said. Full of herself. She got off four stops ahead of him. Neither of them enquired where the other was going.

Eingebildet. • vor

Simon got off on the George IV bridge and walked down the Royal Mile where he met Jake and Angus in the Games Workshop. In the international newsagents Simon lifted three Cadbury's Twirls, a Bounty, a packet of salted peanuts and a can of Irn-Bru, and a *Paris Match* just for the hell of it. After a lot of mindless, spaceless time they moved on and got thrown out of Starbucks. In Bristo Square* they finally got round to skateboarding. Simon didn't have pads or a helmet, no way was he going to wear that stuff where people could see him.

(brit. Spielehersteller mit eigenen Läden) • Zeitungsladen • klaute • (Schokoriegel) • (schott. Softdrink) • (franz. Illustrierte)

info

In Edinburgh werden regelmäßig große Festivals zu unterschiedlichen Themengebieten wie Bücher, Kunst, Film, Wissenschaft etc. veranstaltet. Das **Edinburgh International Festival** findet seit 1947 jedes Jahr für drei Wochen im Spätsommer (meist im August) statt. Es bietet ein vielseitiges Programm aus Klassikkonzerten, Theater, Oper und Tanz mit renommierten Künstlern.

Bristo Square befindet sich etwa anderthalb Kilometer südlich des Stadtzentrums von Edinburgh. Der Platz gehört zum Universitätscampus, ist aber öffentlich zugänglich und bekannt dafür, dass ihn Skateboarder gern nutzen.

liefen umher • Veranstaltungsort • Schafherde

Queen's Hall Festival-goers – what were they like, milling around on the pavement outside the concert venue like a flock of sheep, waiting to be let in. They were all so early, it wasn't like the tickets didn't have seat numbers on, for God's sake. No way was she going to hang around like that. She went for a coffee in a nearby café. A guy came in and sat at the table opposite. Rebecca would lay a bet that he was going to the concert too. She wished it wasn't people like her mother and Beardy Brian who liked classical music. This guy was bearded too. He was drinking a milky coffee and eating some kind of Danish pastry. Apricot. Little flakes of pastry fell into his beard. Gross. The guy was overweight, he shouldn't be eating stuff like that.

hätte darauf wetten können, dass • Blätterteiggebäck • übergewichtig

KO. You Lose. Game Over. Simon flew through the air and heard rather than felt his face slamming into the pavement. A second before that came the 'oh, shit' moment, when you knew it was too late and there was nothing you could do about it. Then the moment when you cast your mind back to the previous second to try to work out what went wrong. Uneven pavement probably. Edinburgh's pavements were crap. Could he have– but no because that moment was past and he

man zurückdenkt an • vorangegangen

Übung 26 Sind die folgenden Aussagen richtig oder falsch? Tragen Sie ein T für true und ein F für false in die Kästchen ein.

1. Rebecca thought that the festival-goers waiting to get into the concert hall were behaving like stupid cows.
2. Rebecca didn't want to join the waiting crowd.
3. Rebecca went for a cup of tea in a nearby tea-room.
4. A good-looking guy sat at the table next to her.
5. The guy was eating some kind of Danish pastry.
6. Rebecca felt attracted to that man.
7. Rebecca would have liked to eat the same thing.

was in the pure empty space of shock. He knew he should enjoy it because it wasn't going to la– too painful to scream so the scream was all inside his head. Jesus, Jesus, Jesus. Jake and Angus bending over him. Jake laughing. 'Good one, bonehead.' Angus not laughing. Angus looking like he was going to boak. 'Jesus, Simon, what a fucking mess.' Passers-by, better equipped with brains, coming to his rescue, thank fuck. Someone wanting him to walk to the A and E, 'It's just a couple of hundred yards, son,' a woman getting all bossy talking about neck collars and fractured skulls. Warm metallic blood in his mouth and all his head rearranged. A doctor appeared, out of breath, he must have run from the hospital.

Simon's phone was in his hand, he had no idea how it got there, the screen was cracked. He gave it to a white-faced Angus. He was gargling blood and there were teeth in his mouth that weren't attached to anything. He held up a finger to Angus and Angus actually understood. 'Speed dial one?' Simon grunted. Speed dial 1. 'MUM' it said on the screen.

Dummkopf • als ob er gleich kotzen würde • Rettung • (= accident and emergency) Notaufnahme • herrisch • Halskrausen • Schädelbrüche

gurgelte

Kurzwahl

The Queen's Hall was packed, the air hot and expectant. That moment of quiet when people gather them-

erwartungsvoll

Übung 27

Bringen Sie die folgenden Sätze in die richtige Reihenfolge.

Simon probably fell because the pavement was uneven.
Simon flew through the air.
A doctor came running to look after him.
His friends were bending over him.
The pain was so overwhelming, he couldn't even cry.
Simon asked his friend to press speed dial 1.
Simon gave his phone to his friend.
Passers-by were giving advice.

selves together and wait. You could power generators on that energy. The Queen's Hall was some kind of church once and you could feel something now, like prayer, willing transformation to occur. Rebecca was standing in the gallery, the cheapest tickets. In the seated parts of the gallery she could see her English teacher, Mr Petrie, from school, looking like he was going to boak (rumour had it that he was dying), Hannah's father with a woman she'd never seen before (file that one away for later), a Gothy couple who looked completely out of place but whom she recognized from somewhere – dressed all in black, him with an Iron Maiden T-shirt, her incredibly fat (how did you get that fat? just by eating?) – and yes indeed, the bearded man from the café, standing on the opposite side of the gallery. Down in the body of the kirk (as you didn't often get to say in a non-metaphorical way), she could see her first music teacher, who she thought was dead, and the boy of her dreams, the Chinese guy who delivered their takeaway (now that *was* interesting).
The four musicians walked on and the quiet changed to stern, energetic applause. Two women, two men, foreign, all funereal, their thoughts in some other, internal universe (perhaps she should have applied to

mit Strom versorgen
durch Willenskraft … geschehen zu lassen • es ging das Gerücht um, dass • zu den Akten legen • (= Gothic) • wiedererkannte
(schott. für) Kirche
ernst • ganz trübsinnig wie auf einer Beerdigung

Übung 28 Ordnen Sie die folgenden Begriffe den jeweiligen Bedeutungsfeldern zu: **Gothy, skull fracture, allegro, funereal, hairline fracture, morphine, ugly, crescendo, bearded, dissonance, dislocated jaw, viola.**

music	medicine	appearance
______	______	______
______	______	______
______	______	______
______	______	______

music college, after all). One woman beautiful, one so-so, both men ugly-ish. No beards. They settled onto their uncomfortable-looking chairs, they adjusted their instruments, they raised their bows – another moment of stillness, absolute this time so that nothing of those first hushed notes of the Adagio would be lost, the cello pulsating on the air, the dissonances building from the violins and the viola – crescendo, drop a step, cello repeating, building, rising, melancholic – Rebecca felt as if she might be about to have a vision, her whole body had lifted a few inches into the air. Only when the sweetness of the Allegro took over, drenching everyone and everything in sunshine, could she relax, safe in the knowledge she wasn't going to float away. The world could not end as long as the 'Dissonant Quartet' was being played.

Bögen
leise
die von … aufgebaut wurden • einen Takt langsamer • als ob sie gleich eine … haben würde • die … tauchte

'Dislocated jaw, broken nose, fractured left cheekbone, hairline fracture to the skull, front teeth gone, bit of your tongue gone – nasty one, that – try to put your hands out to save yourself next time, better still wear the right gear. We'll have to keep you in, obviously, keep an eye on the skull fracture, you don't feel sick at all? Seeing double? Good. Any questions?'
'More morphine?' Except what came out of his mouth didn't sound like language.
'Ha, ha. I'll leave you with Mum now.' The blur of white coat disappeared. *Don't try to talk, darling.* Cool hand stroking his forehead, hot tears rolling down the sides of his face, pooling in his ears. *Everything's all right. Don't talk.* He held his mother's hand. *Hush.*

ausgerenkt • Kiefer • Fissur
Ausrüstung
undeutliches Bild
sammelten sich

And then the Allegro molto. And it was all about closing now and trying to make the most of it because it would finish and really you just wanted it to go on for ever – the bearded man from the café was staring goggle-eyed at her. She closed her eyes. Idiot. But … she opened her eyes. He was clutching his chest, rigid

starrte sie so an, dass ihm fast die Augen aus dem Kopf fielen with terror. He looked as if he might be about to fall headlong over the rail but he staggered into the person next to him, who glared silently in that middle-class way. Rebecca moved fast, round the back of the gallery. By the time she reached him someone had helped him out but he had only got as far as the top of the stairs outside the exit, where he sat now like a man who wasn't accustomed to sitting on stairs. He looked peculiarly unloved. And then he slumped, to a little gasp from the people trying to minister to him. An usher said she'd phoned for an ambulance, someone felt ineffectually for a pulse. The man was the colour of newly poured concrete. Someone was obviously going to have to do something.

'Undo his collar and tie, loosen his belt,' Rebecca said. People looked at her warily. 'It's OK, I'm a trained first-aider,' she snapped. Which was true. She felt with two fingers for the pulse in his neck. Nothing. She checked his chest for breath-signs. Nothing. She tilted his head back and exhaled into his mouth. She could taste coffee and sugar, she could taste the apricot pastry. Gross. She compressed his chest, one-two-three-four-five, one breath, one-two-three-four-five compressions, one breath. She squeezed his heart and gave him her breath and kept on doing so because he wasn't coming back to life like he was supposed to.

The Coda opened – the man was dying to the accompaniment of Mozart – sublime cadence fell on sublime cadence. If she had to die, Rebecca hoped it would be to Mozart. The final cadence, the quick clean ending and then the applause flooding the out-of-sight auditorium. You wouldn't want to die to the sound of applause. A paramedic ran up the stairs towards her. 'Heart attack,' she said, matter-of-factly, between breaths, between compressions. He spoke television dialogue to her, 'I'll take over from here,' and she stood up, suddenly dizzy.

More television dialogue – 'I've got a pulse,' the para-

kopfüber • starrte

nicht gewohnt war, … zu • eigenartig • sackte … zusammen • hörbares Einatmen • sich um … zu kümmern • Platzanweiserin • gegossener • Beton • öffnet • misstrauisch • Ersthelferin • schnauzte • atmete aus • drückte auf • presste • es tun sollte • (Schluss oder Anhang eines musikalischen Satzes) • zur Begleitung von • erhaben • Sanitäter

schwindlig

medic said, glancing up at Rebecca, 'well done.' People murmured praise, someone asked her if she was OK, but she was already gone, stumbling down the stairs, her own healthy heart thudding, out of the door into fine rain and a weak, watery sun and the traffic jammed on Clerk Street. She could hardly breathe, as if the bearded man had taken all of her breath and left her none. She thought she was giving him the gift of life but now it felt as if it was the other way round. And anyway she wasn't sure she wanted the gift of life. Or the gift of death. She didn't want that kind of power, she didn't want to be like a god. What the fuck would she do with that kind of responsibility? She walked quickly, the tears rolling down her face, unchecked.

thudding – schlug dumpf
gift – Geschenk
unchecked – unkontrolliert

Übung 29

Setzen Sie die in Klammern angegebenen Verben ins simple past.

1. An usher __________ (say) she'd phoned for an ambulance.
2. Someone __________ (feel) for a pulse.
3. Rebecca __________ (squeeze) the man's heart and __________ (give) him her breath.
4. She __________ (keep) on doing so, even though it __________ (not, do) really seem to work.
5. When Rebecca finally __________ (stand up), she was dizzy.

I sing of Artemis, whose shafts are of gold,
who cheers on the hounds, the pure maiden
shooter of stags, who delights in archery.

HOMERIC HYMN TO ARTEMIS

Unseen Translation

They had managed an entire afternoon in the Bird Gallery. From egg to skeleton, from common to extinct, from flightless to free, Missy and Arthur were on familiar terms with the avian world.

'Can we come back and do mammals tomorrow?' Arthur asked.

'If you like. There are a lot of them though, remember. You might want to subdivide them into categories.'

'There were a lot of birds. We didn't subdivide them.'

'True.'

Missy believed that knowledge was best taken in small, digestible portions. Museums and galleries, in her opinion, were full of people wandering listlessly from exhibit to exhibit, their eyes glazed over with too much information and not enough knowledge.

'It's an established neurological fact,' Missy told Arthur (Missy believed in using long words with children wherever possible), 'that window shopping and museums are the two most tiring activities for the brain. A chronic insomniac could probably come into the Natural History Museum and fall asleep before he'd got past the diplodocus in the Central Hall.'

Arthur yawned.

'I've noticed you're very suggestible, Arthur.'

'Is that bad?'

'No, it's a good thing, it makes my job much easier. Just make sure it's me that you take suggestions from, not someone else.' The words 'like your mother' remained unspoken, but understood, between them.

The Natural History Museum was closing, already echoing with emptiness and a promise of the secret life it led when no one was there. Missy imagined the

ausgestorben • flugunfähig • waren vertraut mit • Vogelwelt • Säugetiere • unterteilen

teilnahmslos • Ausstellungsstück

Schaufensterbummel • Person, die an Schlaflosigkeit leidet

beeinflussbar

blieben

birds shaking out their feathers and shuffling from one stiff leg to the other, cracking neck bones and easing off flight muscles. Diplodocus himself gave a little tidal tremor along the vertebrae of his huge backbone as if warming up for a leisurely evening stroll. They took no notice of him. Missy never bothered her charges too much with dinosaurs. She thought children (not to mention parents) were far too obsessed with them already.

Outside, the threat of summer rain had darkened the South Kensington sky to an otherworldly purple.

'Are we going home?' Arthur asked, rather indifferently.

'No, we're going to Patisserie Valerie for hot chocolate and cake. Unless you don't like that idea.'

'Ha, ha.'

Missy and Arthur had spent Arthur's school holidays picking and choosing from the capital's smorgasbord of culture. This week, for example, had begun with a short visit to the British Museum* (where they spent most of their time admiring Jennings Dog*), followed on Tuesday by a Mozart String Quartet at the Wigmore Hall*, Wednesday was Shakespeare in the Park (*As You Like It* – 'Very good' in Arthur's opinion) and

ließen … knacken • Halswirbel • entspannten • wie eine Welle • Zittern • Wirbel • Spaziergang • belästigte • die Kinder, die sie betreute • besessen • Regengefahr • (westl. Stadtbezirk von London) • (Kaffeehauskette) • bunte Mischung von • („Wie es euch gefällt" – Theaterstück von William Shakespeare)

info

Das **British Museum** in London ist das weltweit größte Museum zur Kulturgeschichte der Menschheit. **Jennings Dog** ist eine römische Skulptur eines Hundes. Ihren Namen verdankt sie ihrem ersten neuzeitlichen Besitzer.

Die **Wigmore Hall** gilt wegen ihrer hervorragenden Akkustik als einer der besten Konzertsäle der Welt, vor allem für Kammermusik.

Die **National Gallery** liegt am nördlichen Ende des Trafalgar Square. Die staatliche Gemäldesammlung umfasst rund 2300 Werke vom 13. bis 19. Jahrhundert.

yesterday it had been the eighteenth-century rooms of the National Gallery*. Missy was pleased to find that Arthur was able to spend almost twenty minutes in near-silent contemplation of *Whistlejacket**. It was at that moment, as they sat companionably together considering Stubbs's* huge ideal of a horse ('Essence of horse,' Missy whispered in Arthur's ear), that Missy knew for certain that Arthur was a superior version of an eight-year-old boy.

Unfortunately, children were usually spoilt for life by the time Missy got her hands on them. At two years old they had acquired all the faults that would mar them for ever and Missy had to spend most of her time rectifying their old bad habits rather than instilling new good ones. Of course, that was why Missy was called in. She had a reputation, like a Jesuitical troubleshooter, a Marine Corps Mary Poppins* – when all else failed, call in Missy Clark. They expected her to drop in from the skies on the end of an umbrella, like a parachutist floating into a country in the middle of a civil war, and rescue their children from bad behaviour.

Missy was tiring of this phase of her life. She was even thinking of returning to nursing, although not to the hellish half-world of the NHS. She was considering

Betrachtung

waren … verdorben • hatten … angenommen • würden … verunstalten • zu korrigieren • beizubringen • Schlichter

Fallschirmspringer

wurde … müde

Whistlejacket ist der Name eines Pferdes, das der englische Maler und Wissenschaftler George **Stubbs** in einem Gemälde ca. 1760 festhielt. Stubbs (1724–1806) gilt als einer der bedeutendsten europäischen Maler von Tieren.

Mary Poppins, ein Kindermädchen, das magische Fähigkeiten besitzt, ist die Hauptfigur von mehreren Büchern der australischen Schriftstellerin P. L. Travers (1899–1996). Die Geschichte wurde 1964 verfilmt.

applying to a private clinic somewhere, plastic surgery perhaps – somewhere where people weren't actually ill. If she was to remain in this job beyond the age of forty (she was thirty-eight – a difficult age) then she needed a completely blank canvas on which to practise her art. A tabula rasa, untouched by another's hand. A new baby. That was what Romney Wright had offered. A baby so untouched that it wasn't even born yet.

Missy was never interviewed by an employer, she interviewed them. Not that she was looking for the perfect family – years of experience had taught her there was no such thing. All she wanted was a family capable of reformation, and failing that, then just one child in the family who could be rescued from the fate which awaited it (ordinariness). Missy made it a rule never to stay anywhere longer than two years.

'Think of me as the SAS,' she said brightly, when the hugely pregnant Romney had engaged her two weeks before the birth of her second child. Romney – sometime wife of a rock star, glamour model and ironic game-show guest, 'now concentrating on her acting career', but mostly famous for being famous – forgot to mention the first child until Missy was dictating her non-negotiable terms and conditions (own bed-

Schönheitschirurgie
Leinwand
fähig zur
bewahrt werden konnte vor • Schicksal • Gewöhnlichkeit • (= Special Air Service) Spezialeinheit der brit. Armee
nicht verhandelbar

Übung 30 Welches Relativpronomen gehört jeweils in die Lücke – who oder which?

1. Missy was dictating conditions ____________ were non-negotiable.
2. She wanted to work with a child ____________ could be rescued from its fate.
3. Missy had a rule ____________ was to leave after two years.
4. She liked children ____________ didn't talk when they had nothing to say.
5. Romney had an accent ____________ was typical of East London.

room, kitchen, bathroom and sitting room; own car; one and a half days off a week; no nights; full-time maternity nurses for the first three months; pension allowance). In fact, it was only by chance that Arthur wandered into the room at that moment and asked Romney if anyone was going to make his tea or should he heat up some baked beans? Missy was pleased at this – she liked to see a self-sufficient child and had nothing against baked beans.

Säuglingsschwestern • Zulage • zufällig

'Oh, and, of course, this is Arthur,' Romney said carelessly in a grating kind of East London accent that was already beginning to annoy Missy. Hadn't elocution lessons been on the curriculum at Romney's stage school?

krächzend • zu nerven • Sprechtechnik

Missy did actually know about Arthur's existence as she had checked out Romney's (entirely tabloid) cuttings file ('My love for my little boy', 'My single-parent hell', and so on) before arriving at Romney's Primrose Hill house.

'This is the new nanny, Arthur,' Romney said.

aus der Boulevardpresse • Zeitungsausschnitte • (bei Prominenten beliebter Stadtteil Londons) • Kindermädchen

'Oh,' Arthur said, raising surprised eyebrows. Missy liked a child who didn't speak when he had nothing to say.

'Missy,' Missy said to Arthur.

'Missy?' Romney repeated thoughtfully. 'What kind of a name is that?'

'A nickname my father gave me. It stuck.'

'Right. Well, Arthur's called Arthur because his dad was into like Camelot and all that stuff.'

(Sage um König Artus)

'I think it's a very good name,' Missy said, smiling encouragingly at Arthur.

'It's a bit old-fashioned though, isn't it?' Romney frowned. 'I mean "Arthur Wright" sounds like your grandad or something. But that was his dad all over, thought it was funny. His dad's Campbell Wright? Lead singer with Boak? Useless piece of Scottish string. Completely debauched, the lot of them.' Romney pronounced 'debauched' with relish as if it was

Nichtsnutz • verkommen • Genuss

only recently learned. Arthur, a solemn, bespectacled boy, said nothing. Missy had already looked up Boak on the internet. Romney was surprisingly accurate in her choice of vocabulary. Boak were debauched. In photographs they all wore Second World War gas masks, so it was impossible to see if Arthur looked like his father. He certainly didn't resemble his mother, at least not in any major particular, perhaps in the whorl of an ear, the oval of a nostril, nothing too relevant.

'What would you have called him?' Missy asked, intrigued by the idea that you could be the mother of a child and not name it.

'Zeus,' Romney said, without hesitation.

'Zeus?'

'King of the gods,' Romney explained helpfully. Arthur looked at Missy with absolutely no expression on his face. Missy liked a child who kept his own counsel.

'He wears glasses, of course.' Romney sighed. 'Arthur, not Zeus, obviously. When I was a kid,' she carried on, when neither Arthur nor Missy had anything to add to this observation, 'if you wore glasses you were like "speccy four-eyes" or "double-glazing" but now it's cool, like because of Harry Potter. And that kid in that Tom Cruise film. Or no, maybe not him, I don't think that kid was cool, was he? Of course, Campbell was very romantic then, now he's a wanker, but you should have seen our wedding – he planned it all himself – in a ruined castle, I rode over the drawbridge on a white horse and when we were pronounced man and wife – although it wasn't really a vicar, it was more of a shaman kind of bloke – they released butterflies, hundreds of butterflies, over our heads. It was really something, I never thought–'

Missy stood up abruptly; she could see that Romney was a talker. 'I have to go now,' she said. 'When would you like me to start?'

'Tomorrow,' Arthur said promptly. Missy was pleased

kürzlich • eine Brille tragend
sah nicht seiner … ähnlich • in keinem wesentlichen Merkmal • Windung • fasziniert von
seine Meinung für sich behielt
Brillenschlange • Doppelverglasung
Typ • ließen … frei

to hear that he spoke a more civilized form of the English language than his mother.
'He's a funny one, isn't he?' Romney said, for no particular reason.

Missy allowed Arthur two cakes with his hot chocolate. She understood that sometimes one simply wasn't enough.
'What do you think she'll call the baby?' Arthur asked.
'Who are we talking about – the cat's mother? Wipe your fingers.'
'You know who I mean. I bet it's something stupid.'
Romney had been delivered of a baby girl the previous day and Missy and Arthur had visited her that morning in the hospital, in the private maternity wing that was like a five-star hotel. Romney had opted to be knocked unconscious and split open rather than give birth naturally. Missy favoured natural childbirth wherever possible. She thought it was character-forming for a child to have to fight its way into existence. Missy herself was a twin and had made sure she'd elbowed her way out first, ahead of her brother.
The father of Romney's baby was a multi-millionaire, Swiss-born financier who had led an impeccably bor-

zu • (Ermahnung dazu, den Namen einer Person zu nennen) • wisch … ab • hatte sich dafür entschieden • sich bewusstlos schlagen zu lassen (für: Vollnarkose) • aufschneiden zu lassen • sie hatte sich … hinausgedrängelt • makellos

Übung 31

In allen gesuchten Wörtern steckt der Buchstabe „e". Finden Sie die englischen Begriffe anhand der Umschreibungen.

1. a guy ___ ___ ___ ___ e
2. not long ago ___ e ___ e ___ ___ ___ ___
3. wearing glasses ___ e ___ ___ e ___ ___ ___ ___ ___ ___ e ___
4. perfectly ___ ___ ___ e ___ ___ ___ ___ ___ ___
5. to clean by using a cloth ___ ___ ___ e
6. to look like ___ e ___ e ___ ___ ___ e
7. fascinated ___ ___ ___ ___ ___ ___ ___ e ___

ing life until a lifelong interest in West End musicals had led him to bankroll a doomed stage version of Charlotte Brontë's *Villette* in which Romney had a small and surprisingly naked part. In a moment of champagne-and-cocaine-fuelled incontinence at the opening night party, the Swiss financier had found himself in a backstage dressing-room toilet having frantic sex with Romney – a fact which he subsequently vehemently denied when it became tabloid knowledge. ('"I am a love god!" Otto shouted in our steamy sex session.') Romney was now looking forward to the DNA tests to see just how wealthy Otto's seed would prove.

'I'm glad it's a girl,' Arthur said, finishing off his second cake (both his chosen cakes had been chocolate). 'I like girls. Do you know I used to have a male nanny once?'

'And? Was he all right?'

'So-so. He was Australian.'

'How many nannies have you had, Arthur?'

'Five. I think.'

'Why do they leave? Not because of you, you're not a difficult child.'

'Thank you.'

'What about the last one, my predecessor?'

to bankroll – zu finanzieren • doomed – zum Scheitern verurteilt • Charlotte Brontë – (engl. Schriftstellerin, 1816-1855) • fuelled – von … angeheizt • frantic – wild • steamy – heiß • wealthy – reich • would prove – sich erweisen würde • predecessor – Vorgängerin

Übung 32

Die folgenden Wörter bedeuten das Gegenteil von Wörtern auf dieser Doppelseite. Tragen Sie die Begriffe aus dem Text ein.

1. poor ____________________
2. female ____________________
3. successor ____________________
4. easy ____________________
5. gladly ____________________
6. irrelevant ____________________
7. successful ____________________

Arthur shrugged.
'What does that mean? The shrugging?'
Arthur stood up and piled their dirty plates neatly. 'We should go. The tube's going to be packed.'
The rain held off as they walked to the underground. Missy thought it was important for a child to use public transport, to suffer dreary queues and biting winds. Even when working for the richest families she had made a point of hauling their children around the streets of London on buses and tubes and trains. She believed stoicism was a virtue that was badly in need of reviving.
They went into a newsagent's so that Missy could replenish essentials – she was never without Elastoplasts, safety pins, first-class stamps, tissues, extra-strong mints, Nurofen, cough sweets, Calpol, bottled water. The search for tissues led them past the newspaper and magazine racks which took up one wall. All of the top shelf was occupied by glossy girls presenting their buttocks or breasts to the camera.
'Difficult though it may be for you to believe, one day, sadly, you will probably find these images attractive,' Missy told Arthur. 'But for now you can buy a *Beano*.'
Arthur wasn't listening. 'Look,' he said, pointing to

stapelte … aufeinander • (Londoner) U-Bahn • trostlos • hatte … Wert darauf gelegt • zu schleppen • Tugend • dringend • wiederbelebt werden musste • wiederaufstocken konnte • (Klebepflaster) • (Schmerzmittel) • Hustenbonbons • (Schmerzmittel) • Regale • Hintern • (Comiczeitschrift für Kinder)

Übung 33

Vervollständigen Sie die Sätze, indem Sie die Buchstaben in den Klammern in die richtige Reihenfolge bringen.

1. The magazines on the top shelf had cover girls who were showing their ________________ (tubokstc).
2. Romney hoped Otto's seed would ________________ (rovpe) to be wealthy.
3. A lot was written about Romney's affair in the ________________ (ltaodsib).
4. Arthur ____________ (dilpe) the dirty dishes neatly.
5. For Missy, stoicism was a ______________ (eitvru).

the rack of tabloids beneath the naked women. Nearly every newspaper had a photograph of Romney Wright on the front, posing in her hospital bed – 'Romney's bundle of joy', '**Love-rat** leaves Romney holding the baby', 'Romney **keeping mum about** dad' (which was hardly true). Romney had managed to adopt a pose similar to the models in the pornographic magazines – her huge, milk-swollen breasts offered to the camera like gifts. The baby itself seemed **incidental**, almost invisible inside its **shawl cocoon**. Arthur **skim-read** the text. 'They don't mention me,' he said.

'That's a good thing.'

'I know.' Arthur **gazed at** the photographs of his mother as if she was an interesting stranger. 'Do you think we'll like the baby?'

'What's not to like?'

Arthur gazed at his **overexposed** mother. Missy liked a wise child better than anyone but she considered the expression on Arthur's face to be **knowledgeable well beyond his years**.

'I realize you've already had far too much chocolate today and **are** probably **as high as a kite**, which is a technical term used by nannies, but, and against my better judgement, and you will rarely hear those words

untreuer Mann • schweigt über • nebensächlich • Tuch • Kokon • überflog • betrachtete • zur Schau gestellt • viel zu wissend für sein Alter • bist … total high

Übung 34 Welche Aussagen über Arthur stimmen? Kreuzen Sie die richtigen an.

- ☐ He is not sure if he'll like the new baby.
- ☐ He doesn't look at the magazines with his mother's picture on the cover.
- ☐ Chocolate is one of his favourite sweets.
- ☐ He is quite naïve for an eight-year-old boy.
- ☐ He is afraid of the myth about Artemis.
- ☐ He would have named his sister "Jane".
- ☐ He reads the article about his mum carefully.

from my lips, Arthur, you can have a packet of chocolate buttons. Now come on, don't dawdle.'

Schokolinsen • trödel nicht

✶

The baby was finally named. Romney toyed with a galaxy of goddesses ('Athene? Aphrodite? Artemis?') and gave up before reaching the end of the alphas.

'What did they do?' Arthur asked as they meandered ('from the river god Maeander, by the way') through the textile rooms of the V and A.

'Well,' Missy said, 'Athene was smug and thought she knew everything, Aphrodite was a troublemaker, and very irritating, I might add, and only Artemis had any sense.'

'What did she do?'

'Virgin, close relationship with the moon, childbirth, wolves. Oh, and the chase.'

'The chase?'

'Shot stags with silver arrows, that kind of thing.'

umherschlenderten • Wandteppichsammlung • (= Victoria and Albert Museum: Kunst- und Designmuseum) • selbstgefällig • Jagd

Hirsche

Arthur looked horrified. 'Shot stags?' he echoed ('from Echo – an unfortunate nymph. Show me one that isn't').

'It's a mythic thing, no stags were actually harmed during the … that kind of thing.'

Romney had offered the choice of name to Arthur but reneged when he opted for 'Jane', a name far too plain for Romney's tastes. In the end, she went for world geography. Romney's sister Johdi had a child called Africa and her friend Lily had a baby called India so Romney decided on China for Arthur's sister. 'Like collecting countries,' she said to Missy. 'They'll be like NATO or something when they grow up.'

hatte nicht … Wort gehalten

'It could have been much worse,' Missy said to Arthur. 'Belgium, Luxemburg, New Zealand, Gibraltar, Uzbekistan. The list of worse is endless. That's not grammatical, by the way.'

China, although in no way Chinese, was as delicate as

zart

porcelain with creamy skin and a rosy blush on her cheeks. She was more robust than her name implied but nevertheless received round-the-clock attention from a series of maternity nurses who themselves received round-the-clock attention from the nanny-cam in the nursery. Romney had a monitor in her bedroom so that she could watch the nurse watching her baby. Otto's DNA had finally been forced to own up as the culprit ('Kraut comes clean – "China's mine" ') much to Romney's relief, although, 'He wasn't a kraut,' she said indignantly.

war ... gezwungen gewesen • zuzugeben • Übeltäter • (abwertende Bezeichnung für einen Deutschen) • beichtet • Erleichterung • entrüstet • war gesättigt mit • stämmig

Autumn came. The Primrose Hill household was running smoothly – Romney was sated with money and sex, the sex in the stocky form of a soap star, Arthur was as happy as an eight-year-old boy can be at school ('OK, I suppose') and China was a dream of a child. Even the tabloid photographers had stopped camping on the doorstep and Missy was looking forward to the school break and some leaf-kicking time in London's parks with Arthur and the baby, when Romney suddenly announced that Arthur was going to visit his father for half-term.

Schulferien (nach ca. der Hälfte eines Trimesters) • gemeinsames Sorgerecht • aus gekochten Eiern • leichte Mahlzeit am Nachmittag

'They have joint custody,' Arthur explained over a boiled-egg tea down in the huge basement kitchen.
'And when did you last see him?'
Arthur thought for a long time. 'Two years ago, I think. You have to come with me,' he added matter-of-factly.
'Why?'
'Because he's on tour.'
'On tour?'

'Oh yeah, didn't I say?' Romney said when Missy questioned her. 'Boak are in the middle of like this huge world tour, actually I think they're always on it. Arthur's going to visit him when they're in Germany.

Flying into Munich, flying out of Hamburg at the end of the week. All the arrangements have been made by his publicist, you're going too. And I tell you what, I'm going to give you your own credit card. How's that? One more thing for the kraut to pay for.'

'He's Swiss,' Missy reminded her.

'Same difference,' Romney said.

Pressesprecherin

'What about my hamster?' Arthur asked Missy.

'We'll ask Africa to look after him.'

'What about the baby?'

'It's only a week,' Missy said, 'and babies are almost indestructible, you know.' Romney, however, decided not to look after China herself but to go on a 'detox meditation' in the Cotswolds with her friend Lily while China went to stay with her maternal grandmother, who had, in Romney's words, 'been dying to get a shot at her'.

'So China will be fine,' Missy reassured Arthur. 'After all, your grandmother managed to bring your mother up.' Arthur gave Missy the most beautifully blank look.

'You can be very enigmatic sometimes, Arthur,' Missy said ('from the Greek *ainigma*, derived from *ainos* – fable').

Entgiftungs- • (hügelige Region in Mittelwestengland) • Großmutter mütterlicherseits • darauf brannte • sich an … zu versuchen • hintergründig

Übung 35

Bei welchen der markierten Satzteile gehören Bindestriche zwischen die Wörter, bei welchen nicht? Setzen Sie sie dort, wo sie hingehören.

1. The baby received round the clock attention.
2. The Primrose Hill household was running smoothly.
3. Arthur's parents have joint custody.
4. Romney wants to go on a detox meditation.
5. The band was on a world tour.
6. Arthur told Missy matter of factly that she had to stay with him.
7. Missy was looking forward to some leaf kicking time.

an … teilzuhaben • gleichgültig • (3.-Welt-Laden, der Second-Hand-Artikel verkauft)

If they were on their way to partake of Boak's debauchery, there was no indication of it in Lufthansa business class, which was so clean and grey and lacking in decadence that Arthur, a nonchalant traveller, managed to study the Collins German phrase book that Missy had bought him in an Oxfam shop prior to the trip ('Why buy new?' she said to Arthur, 'when you can buy cheap?') while Missy herself read a book about astronomy that she had taken out from the library. Missy thought it was important to use libraries. ('Why buy at all when you can borrow?') She wasn't particularly interested in astronomy but she believed an important part of her job was to impart as much general knowledge as possible to her charges, because if not her, then who?

'Did you know,' Missy asked Arthur, 'that they can weigh galaxies?'

'Sie führen mich an,' Arthur said, consulting his phrase book.

'I'm sorry?'

'You're pulling my leg,' he laughed, pleased that he knew something that Missy didn't.

waren im Besitz von • Reiseablauf • Etappe

Missy and Arthur were in possession of an extraordinarily detailed itinerary for the German leg of Boak's

Übung 36 Setzen Sie in die Lücken **if** oder **when** ein.

1. There was no taxi at the airport ________ they arrived.
2. ________ there was a reservation for them, the receptionist should know.
3. ________ I can find a second-hand book, I won't buy a new one.
4. Why should I buy a new book ________ I know I can get the same one cheaper in an Oxfam shop?
5. ________ Missy didn't care for Arthur, then who would?
6. ________ this was to be the luxury life they had dreamed of, then it was not very impressive.

tour, prepared by the band's publicist, a girl called Lulu, who, as well as providing flight times, driver details and hotel reservations, had also given two different mobile numbers on which she could be contacted. The itinerary also informed them that they were going to travel around Germany on Boak's tour bus.
'What will that be like?' Missy asked Arthur, as the plane bumped lightly onto the runway at Munich airport. Arthur frowned, carefully searching for the right word.
'Extreme,' he said finally.

zur Verfügung gestellt hatte • Handy

setzte auf

There was no car to collect them at the airport, as promised by Lulu, but Missy had changed sterling into Deutschmarks at Heathrow and they caught a taxi to the hotel with the careless abandon of people on someone else's expenses.
The Bayerischer Hof had no record of any reservation.
'Two rooms? In the name of Wright?' Missy persisted, showing the receptionist Lulu's careful itinerary. The receptionist regarded it politely as if it was a document from another civilization, far away in time and space, and beyond translation.
'Are Boak actually staying here?' Missy asked, wishing

Pfund (brit. Währung) • (internationaler Flughafen in London) • Unbekümmertheit • auf Kosten eines anderen • Beleg • höflich • unübersetzbar

Übung 37

Bilden Sie eine Wörterkette mit den englischen Übersetzungen folgender Begriffe, die hier allerdings in anderer Reihenfolge stehen:

Mädchen – Unbekümmertheit – Büchereien – Pfund – Etappe – Reisen – gleichgültig

Der letzte Buchstabe eines Wortes und der Anfangsbuchstabe des nächsten Wortes sind jeweils gleich.

_ _ _ _ _ _ n n _ _ _ _ _ _ _ _ _ t

t _ _ _ _ _ _ _ g _ _ _ _

l _ _ _ _ _ _ _ _ _ _ _ _ _ _ _ _ _

they weren't called such a stupid name. At first, the receptionist thought she was trying to say 'book' and then 'Björk'. The smile on the receptionist's face grew stiff and tired. She called the manager.

'What does boak mean, anyway?' Missy asked Arthur as they waited.

'It's Scottish for sick.'

'Ill sick or vomit sick?'

'Vomit sick.'

The manager appeared, smiling sadly, and said that he very much regretted but the hotel never revealed details about its guests. It was growing late by now and Missy felt an uncharacteristic reluctance for battle. Arthur was sitting on their luggage, looking like a weary refugee, and Missy decided they would take a room anyway. She offered the brand-new gold credit card Romney had given her before they left. A few minutes later the hotel manager returned it to her and said in a low murmur that he was very sorry but the card was 'not acceptable'. He smiled even more sadly. Missy paid for the room on her own card.

'How much money do you have?' Arthur asked.

'Quite a lot actually,' Missy said truthfully. 'I've been saving for years.'

krank im Sinne von „mir ist nicht gut" • krank im Sinne von „erbrechen müssen" • gebe … preis • Widerwillen • Kampf • erschöpft • Flüchtling

Übung 38 Arthur gibt ein paar Kommentare auf Deutsch ab. Verbinden Sie die deutschen Aussprüche mit den englischen Entsprechungen.

„Das ist Pech."	„What a pity."
„Es sind schlechte Zeiten."	„Did anyone ask for us?"
„Wie schade."	„Bad luck."
„Hat jemand nach uns gefragt?"	„These are bad times."

'But you're not supposed to be paying.'
'True. But it's only for one night. I expect your father'll turn up tomorrow.'
'Das ist Pech,' Arthur consoled.

The room was nice, although not the 'luxury suite' promised by Lulu. The floors were clean and the sheets snappy with starch. Missy ordered cheese omelettes and apfelstrudel on room service. After they had eaten she phoned both the mobile numbers that Lulu had provided. One was completely dead, the other announced something impenetrable in a German that was well beyond the capacity of the phrase book. Missy phoned Romney's Primrose Hill number but there was no answer. On Romney's mobile a voice announced that it might not be switched on.

Laken • starr vor Stärke

They filled in their breakfast cards – Arthur found this very exciting – and then watched an incomprehensible game show on television that even if they had been fluent in German they probably wouldn't have understood. They went to their beds at nine o'clock German time, eight o'clock Primrose Hill time, and they both slept as soundly as babies until the maid hammered on the door with their breakfast, long after the dawn had scattered her yellow robes across the skies.

unverständlich

schliefen so fest wie • gestreut hatte

After breakfast, which Arthur liked almost as much as the ordering of it, Missy tried all the phone numbers she had tried the previous evening, with the same result. 'Es sind schlechte Zeiten,' Arthur said, leafing industriously through his phrase book. 'Wie schade.'

eifrig

Missy went down to reception and looked the sadly smiling manager in the eye in the same way that she looked at little boys when she particularly wanted them to tell her the truth.
'If you were me,' she said to him, 'and think about this carefully, would you stay another night in this unbelievably expensive hotel and wait for the band known, unfortunately, as Boak to turn up?'

'No,' he said, 'I wouldn't.'
'Thank you.'

sieh's mal so • uns amüsieren

'Look at it this way,' Missy said to Arthur. 'Our flight from Hamburg isn't for another week, we have enough money – even if it's mine – and we are in one of the great cultural cities of Western Europe in the half-term holidays, so we may as well enjoy ourselves.'

nicht … aufgetaucht waren

They moved into a guest house on Karlstrasse, although they returned several times to the Bayerischer Hof to check that Boak hadn't suddenly materialized. 'Hat jemand nach uns gefragt?' Arthur asked the sad manager. No, he replied, in English, they hadn't.

durchgestrichen • Großbuchstaben

They trekked to the Olympiahalle and discovered a tour poster slashed with a banner in large red capitals, declaring that Boak's concert was 'Entfällt'.

absolut

'I think that means cancelled,' Arthur said without bothering to consult the German dictionary they'd bought ('Sometimes you have no choice but to buy'). After that, they didn't bother returning to the Bayerischer Hof. Lulu and Romney remained unreachable by all means.

'Perhaps we're dead,' Arthur suggested, 'and we just don't know it.'

abstrus

'I think that's a rather fanciful explanation,' Missy said.

in Übereinstimmung mit • in Maßen • vor dem 16. Jahrhundert entstanden • innerhalb von

In accord with Missy's beliefs, they visited museums and galleries in moderation – the Forum der Technik (but only the Planetarium), the Deutsches Museum (but only the coal mine), the Alte Pinakothek (but only presixteenth-century paintings). Arthur stayed awake for the whole of the BMW museum – he wasn't an eight-year-old boy for nothing – but was asleep on his feet within minutes of going into the Residenz-Museum. The Frauenkirche and the Peterskirche had much the same effect on both of them. An expedition to the Schloss Nymphenburg might have been more of a success if it hadn't rained so much. Their favourite museum exhibit was a chance discovery, a stuffed creature, in the oddly named Jagd-und Fischereimuseum ('Hunting and fishing,' Arthur supplied helpfully). The 'Wolpertinger' was a curious Mitteleuropean chimera, a mix of rabbit, stag and duck, plus something less definable and more frightening. ('Distantly related to the rare wolfkin,' Missy said.)

'Bavarian primeval creature,' Arthur read from the guidebook the sad hotel manager had given them on their last visit to the Bayerischer Hof.

In truth, neither of them was much in the mood for history and culture and they spent a lot of time wandering in the Englischer Garten or drinking hot chocolate. Every day at midday they went and stood ritualistically in front of the glockenspiel on the Neues Rathaus and watched for all the brightly coloured figures to make their rounds.

'What did happen to your last nanny?' Missy asked as they waited for the glockenspiel to start. Arthur made a pinched sort of face.

'What,' Missy encouraged, 'she was murdered? She killed herself, she came back as a ghost and wandered round a lake? Fell in love with the master who had a

Jungwolf • bayerisch • urzeitlich

keiner der beiden war in der richtigen Stimmung für

verkniffen

Vervollständigen Sie die Sätze mit den folgenden Wörtern:

Übung 39

by all means – much – enough – more – large

1. Missy and Arthur had ____________ money to continue their journey.
2. The banner declared its message in ___________ capitals.
3. Lulu and Romney remained unreachable _______________.
4. Neither Arthur nor Missy were _____________ in the mood for history and culture.
5. The "Wolpertinger" looked like a mix of several animals plus something _____________ frightening.

auf dem Dachboden • schrecklich • entstellt

mad wife in the attic and who became hideously disfigured in a fire?'

'You're not supposed to talk like that to eight-year-olds.'

'Sorry.'

'She left.'

'Left?'

'Left. She said she wouldn't leave and she did. And I liked her.' Arthur stuck his hands in his pockets and angrily kicked an imaginary stone on the ground. 'I liked her and she promised she wouldn't leave and she did. And you'll leave.' His face began to quiver and he kicked the ground harder. His shoe was getting scuffed. Missy tried to touch the small shoulders, heaving with suppressed tears, but Arthur grew suddenly hysterical and shook her off.

zu zittern

abgewetzt

'You'll leave just like she did,' he screamed. 'You'll leave me and I hate you! I hate you, I hate you, I hate you!'

'Arthur–'

'Shut up, shut up, shut up!' he yelled, so wound up now that he could hardly breathe, and several passersby regarded with curiosity the small English boy struggling furiously to escape his mother's grip.

Übung 40

Welche der knappen Antworten gehört zu welcher Frage? Tragen Sie den entsprechenden Buchstaben in das Kästchen neben der Frage ein.

1. Where is the ticket sales desk?
2. Who gave Arthur some cake?
3. How long was Arthur sobbing?
4. Why were Arthur's eyes red?
5. When will Arthur leave Missy?
6. Who cried "shut up" several times?
7. Who put Arthur to bed?

'It feels as though we've been away years,' Arthur said when the cab dropped them off at Munich airport.
'I know.'
'Do you think anyone's missed us?'
'Can you see the Lufthansa sales desk?' — Ticketschalter
'Over there.'
Arthur, Missy was relieved to see, was quite calm today, although his eyes were still red from crying – he had sobbed for hours, long after Missy had got him back to the Karlstrasse guest house, long after she had put him to bed with milk and honey cake offered by the sympathetic proprietress. 'Die Kinder,' she sighed, as if to be a child was the worst thing in the world. Arthur had finally fallen asleep, flushed and tear-stained, clutching onto Missy's hand. 'I don't hate you, you know,' he said, with a grief-stricken hiccup. 'I love you really.'

Besitzerin • tränenüberströmt • kummervoll • Schluckauf

'I love you too,' she said, kissing the top of his head, 'and I promise I won't leave you and I never break promises. Ever. You'll leave me one day, though,' she added softly when Arthur was asleep.

They waited in the queue at the ticket sales desk. The airport was hot and incredibly busy. So many airlines,

a) The proprietress of the guesthouse did.
b) Arthur did.
c) Over there.
d) For hours.
e) One day.
f) Missy did.
g) Because he had been crying.

so many destinations. Arthur read them off the departure board: 'Paris, Rome, Lisbon, New York, London Heathrow.'

'I think we should have bought these tickets earlier,' Missy said, looking uncharacteristically distracted. Arthur yawned extravagantly. 'Ich langweile mich,' he said. 'At least I learnt some German.'

abgelenkt

'Yes, you've done very well, Arthur,' Missy said vaguely.

'Are you all right?'

'Mm.'

The Lufthansa sales clerk regarded Missy's request for two single tickets to Hamburg with solemnity. She would gladly sell her them, she said, but all the Hamburg flights were full until that evening, did she still want to go?

Schalterangestellte • mit großem Ernst • ob sie dann trotzdem dort hinwolle

'How about London?' Missy asked.

'I can get you on the next flight to Heathrow,' the sales clerk said, 'but not sitting together.'

'It will be quicker for us just to go straight home,' Missy said to Arthur.

'Mm,' Arthur said.

Missy thought about buying a ticket for London. She thought for rather a long time so that the sales clerk

Übung 41 Alle gesuchten englischen Begriffe fangen mit dem gleichen Buchstaben an. Finden Sie sie mithilfe der Umschreibungen.

1. nevertheless
2. in the near future
3. winding
4. precious metal
5. to cry
6. summer shoes
7. a distinctive noise

grew agitated because of the long queue snaking and coiling and knotting behind Arthur and Missy. | die sich schlängelte • wand • verknotete

'Arthur,' Missy said finally, 'have you ever been to Rome?'

'I don't think so.'

'I can get you on a connecting flight to Rome leaving in half an hour,' the sales clerk said hopefully. | Anschlussflug

'A lot of museums in Rome,' Arthur said.

'A lot,' Missy agreed.

'And there are other places too,' Arthur said.

'Oh, yes,' Missy agreed, 'there are many places. So many places that you need never come back to where you started from.'

'Which was Primrose Hill,' Arthur said. He tugged at Missy's hand. 'What about China?'

'China?' the sales clerk asked, looking agitated.

'Don't panic,' Missy said to her ('from the Great God Pan, now dead, thank goodness'). 'I don't know about China,' Missy said solemnly to Arthur. 'I'm afraid her fate may be to stay with Romney.' | Gott sei Dank

'You're going to have to hurry,' the sales clerk said, 'the gate will be closing soon.'

They ran. They ran so fast Arthur was sure they were going to take off before they even got on the plane. Missy pulled him along by the hand and when he looked at her feet her sensible leather boots had turned into silver sandals and he wondered if that was why they were able to run so fast. The airport tannoy stopped announcing that passengers for Düsseldorf should go to the gate and instead broadcast the rousing sound of a hunting horn. For a few dizzy seconds Arthur saw the quiver of silver arrows on Missy's back, gleaming with moonshine. He saw her green, wolfish eyes light up with amusement as she shouted, 'Come on, Arthur, hurry up,' while a pack of hounds bayed and boiled around her silver-sandalled feet, eager for the chase. | Lautsprecher • mitreißend • Jagdhunde • bellten • tobten • begierig auf

Lösungen

1
to be beaten to a pulp
to carry a child
to give somebody the creeps
to drop dead
to be ridden with allergies
to come across too many accidents
to shrug off one's pathetic fears
to be terrified of having a standard life

2
1. [F] June wasn't allowed to have pets when she was a child.
June durfte als Kind keine Haustiere haben.
2. [F] June had two hamsters, a male and a female one.
June hatte zwei Hamster, ein Männchen und ein Weibchen.
3. [T] **June's parents always feared something awful might happen to their daughter.**
Junes Eltern befürchteten stets, dass ihrer Tochter etwas Schreckliches zustoßen könnte.
4. [F] According to June's mother her husband died of choking on a sweet.
Laut Junes Mutter erstickte ihr Mann an einem Bonbon.
5. [T] **June didn't want to lead an ordinary life.**
June wollte kein gewöhnliches Leben führen.
6. [F] A semi-detached villa in the suburbs was June's dream.
Eine Doppelhaushälfte am Stadtrand war Junes Traum.

3
1. old-fashioned – ~~**modern**~~ – ancient – former
2. snuffle – sneeze – ~~**shuffle**~~ – wheeze
3. decent – nice – neat – ~~**crappy**~~
4. ~~**news**~~ – sitcom – soap opera – comedy
5. bath – bedroom – ~~**en-suite**~~ – kitchen

4
1. Eddie liked to look at the **ultrasound** photograph of the sister he soon would have.
2. Sometimes you have to give something away as a **sacrifice**.
3. Eddie studied the grammar and **stroked** a beard that wasn't there.
4. In the **Botanics** you can see plants and some animals like fish and birds.
5. A frog starts out as a tiny **tadpole**.

5
naoce**ribbons**nanxo**despise**nmuopsgxay**atone**yupsvietnh
sym**crete**clemystawipisym**punishment**qopjefmtuclwpom
eruhpoq**plait**xvnhgorutrommsamwo**achievement**yartuvo

6

		1								4
		a			2					b
		b			m					u
		r	5	t	i	n	n	y		t
		o			d					t
6	h	a	l	l	w	a	y			e
		d			i			3		r
					f			v		f
					e			a		l
								n		y

7

- [X] **June was good at swimming.**
  June konnte gut schwimmen.
- [ ] She had once seen a painting of a dolphin in a Roman villa.
  Sie hatte einmal ein Gemälde von einem Delfin in einer römischen Villa gesehen.
- [X] **June would have liked to turn into a dolphin.**
  June hätte sich gerne in einen Delfin verwandelt.
- [ ] She slowly sank to the seabed.
  Sie sank langsam auf den Meeresgrund.
- [X] **June's parents were afraid their daughter might drown.**
  Junes Eltern befürchteten, ihre Tochter könnte ertrinken.
- [X] **Her parents only went on holiday with her in Great Britain.**
  Ihre Eltern verbrachten jeden Urlaub mit ihr in Großbritannien.
- [ ] June discovered an anchor on the seabed.
  Auf dem Meeresgrund entdeckte June einen Anker.
- [ ] June was on a little boat in the Atlantic.
  June war auf einem kleinen Boot im Atlantik.

8

1. **Stuck up** amongst the plants was a handwritten sign.
2. Eddie knew the sign was not there for him, but nevertheless he couldn't stop **hoping**.
3. She told herself **to think** positively for the sake of her baby.
4. The island was **bathed** in golden sunlight.
5. Hawk fancied **joining** a special community.

9

1. Some people get away **with** almost everything.
2. Only now could Addison understand the reason **for** his visit to his father many years ago.
3. Though Clare didn't believe **in** God, she refrained **from** letting the minister know.
4. Addison found himself standing **at** the altar.
5. He had the strange feeling he had been dropped **into** a totally different life.

10 **1.** As a young boy, Addison was always **hungry**.
Als kleiner Junge war Addison immer hungrig.
2. A **neighbour** often gave Addison something to eat.
Eine Nachbarin gab Addison oft etwas zu essen.
3. Shirley used to wear shoes **with very high heels**.
Shirley trug oft Schuhe mit sehr hohen Absätzen.
4. Shirley had started off the journey in **good spirits.**
Shirley hatte die Reise in guter Laune begonnen.
5. They went to his father's house **on a Sunday**.
Sie gingen an einem Sonntag zum Haus seines Vaters.
6. As a boy, Addison used to **hang around in the streets**.
Als Junge pflegte Addison auf der Straße rumzuhängen.

11 a **melodious** voice
a **wrought-iron** gate
in **agitated** thought
a **striped** dress
a **stiff** collar
booming laughter

12 **1.** Addison was so hungry that his stomach **groaned**.
2. They had never discussed the **subject** beforehand.
3. Clare got pregnant soon after the **wedding**.
4. Shirley gave her son a **critical** look.
5. Shirley said: "Time to confront his **majesty** in all his glory."

13 **1.** awfully, **2.** slack, **3.** intimidate, **4.** prospect, **5.** snotty, **6.** glaikit, **7.** contravention, **8.** rank, **9.** beard

14 **1.** She called out **gaily** to everyone to come to dinner.
2. His face didn't show any emotion and looked like a **glacial** mask.
3. Shirley was observed as if she was a **dangerous** animal.
4. "This is a private house," Bill said **angrily** to Shirley.
5. Shirley was advancing on him rather **aggressively**.

15

Substantiv	Adjektiv
impossibility	**impossible**
trouble	troublesome
solemnity	**solemn**
fatality	fatal
imagination	imaginative
delicacy	delicate
apoplexy	**apoplectic**
dampness	damp
obscenity	obscene

16

1. While the baby was being born, **a woman died in a car crash.**
   Während das Baby geboren wurde, starb eine Frau bei einem Autounfall.
2. In the hospital Addison waited **alone in a small waiting room.**
   Im Krankenhaus wartete Addison allein in einem kleinen Wartezimmer.
3. The new-born child **looked healthier than his mother.**
   Das Neugeborene sah gesünder aus als seine Mutter.
4. Addison and Clare **had five possible names for the baby.**
   Addison und Clare hatten fünf mögliche Namen für das Baby.

17

1. wanting to know everything	**curious**
2. chewing gum can be blown into a	**bubble**
3. burial or cremation of a dead person	**funeral**
4. having a big belly	**paunchy**
5. a person who feels grief or sorrow	**mourner**
6. not well-dressed	**frumpy**
7. not clearly or distinctly	**vaguely**

18

to find	**found**	found
to think	thought	**thought**
to mean	**meant**	meant
to know	**knew**	known
to do	did	**done**
to speak	**spoke**	spoken
to make	made	**made**
to have	had	**had**

19

1. [b] Susan believed that her father had abused her sister, **but she wouldn't talk about it.**
   Susan glaubte, dass ihr Vater ihre Schwester missbraucht hatte, aber diese wollte nicht darüber sprechen.
2. [e] Addison thought about telling her **that his wife had just had a baby.**
   Addison überlegte, ob er ihr erzählen sollte, dass seine Frau gerade ein Baby bekommen hatte.
3. [a] The idea of being a father was still so new **that he might start crying if he talked about it.**
   Die Vorstellung, Vater zu sein, war noch so neu, dass er vielleicht anfangen würde zu weinen, wenn er darüber sprach.
4. [d] When Addison declared that his father was dead **it came out a lot harsher than originally intended.**
   Als Addison sagte, dass sein Vater tot sei, klang es viel barscher, als er eigentlich beabsichtigt hatte.
5. [c] Addison was surprised by his own gesture, **actually a lot more than Susan was.**
   Addison war selbst von seiner Geste überrascht, sogar viel mehr als Susan.

20

n	o	m	s	m	o	o	t	h	i	r	t
m	h	i	p	c	l	r	t	o	o	h	a
e	h	e	v	k	a	n	e	a	t	s	b
x	m	o	a	r	e	z	h	t	u	g	d
c	p	e	t	d	i	t	s	c	m	y	i
e	x	i	y	n	p	v	t	k	u	o	c
p	w	z	b	c	u	h	i	l	q	j	a
t	s	l	e	f	m	g	o	a	e	w	t
o	e	p	q	j	r	e	n	n	v	x	e
c	g	u	i	l	t	y	t	q	e	r	m
x	t	a	s	s	a	u	l	t	l	s	o
a	n	t	o	g	a	l	i	g	n	e	k

21 **curiously** = strangely
leaf through = browse
saggy = flabby
grunt = grumble
fault = failing
messy = untidy

22
1. Rebecca wished her mother would die of a **brain haemorrhage**.
Rebecca wünschte, ihre Mutter würde an einer Hirnblutung sterben.
2. Simon went to bed without bothering to **undress**.
Simon ging zu Bett, ohne sich die Mühe zu machen, sich auszuziehen.
3. Rebecca fell asleep listening to **Bach**.
Rebecca schlief ein, während sie Bach hörte.
4. For Simon and Rebecca, Beardy Brian was **a stranger**.
Für Simon und Rebecca war Beardy Brian ein Fremder.
5. Their mother used to say: "Privileges come with duties **attached**."
Ihre Mutter pflegte zu sagen: "Privilegien sind immer mit Pflichten verbunden."
6. Beardy Brian earns his money as a **social worker**.
Beardy Brian verdient sein Geld als Sozialarbeiter.

23 **1.** **grown-up** **2.** **to snicker** **3.** **resort** **4.** **real ale** **5.** **awkward** **6.** **ridiculous**

24

								6.		
			1.	c	l	a	t	t	e	r
								r		
			4.			5.		e		
			b			d		m		
			r			e		b		7.
2.	g	r	a	t	e	f	u	l		a
			i			l		e		v
			n			a				o
			y			t				i
				3.	r	e	c	o	r	d

25 **1.** illicit (verboten)
Alle anderen Wörter drücken Gefühle des Mitleids und Bedauerns aus.

2. to snuffle (schniefen)
Alle anderen Verben bezeichnen Formen des Lachens.

3. step (Schritt)
Alle anderen Wörter bezeichnen Schläge und Tritte.

26 **1.** [F] Rebecca thought that the festival-goers waiting to get into the concert hall were behaving like stupid cows.
Rebecca fand, dass die Festival-Besucher, die auf Einlass in die Konzerthalle warteten, sich wie dumme Rindviecher benahmen.
2. [T] **Rebecca didn't want to join the waiting crowd.**
Rebecca wollte sich nicht zu der wartenden Menge gesellen.
3. [F] Rebecca went for a cup of tea in a nearby tea-room.
Rebecca ging in eine nahegelegene Teestube, um eine Tasse Tee zu trinken.
4. [F] A good-looking guy sat at the table next to her.
Ein gut aussehender Typ saß am Nachbartisch.
5. [T] **The guy was eating some kind of Danish pastry.**
Der Typ aß irgendein Blätterteiggebäck.
6. [F] Rebecca felt attracted to that man.
Rebecca fühlte sich von dem Mann angezogen.
7. [F] Rebecca would have liked to eat the same thing.
Rebecca hätte gern das gleiche gegessen.

27
[2] Simon probably fell because the pavement was uneven.
[1] Simon flew through the air.
[6] A doctor came running to look after him.
[4] His friends were bending over him.
[3] The pain was so overwhelming, he couldn't even cry.
[8] Simon asked his friend to press speed dial 1.
[7] Simon gave his phone to his friend.
[5] Passers-by were giving advice.

28

music	**medicine**	**appearance**
allegro	skull fracture	Gothy
crescendo	hairline fracture	funereal
dissonance	morphine	ugly
viola	dislocated jaw	bearded

29 **1.** An usher **said** she'd phoned for an ambulance.
2. Someone **felt** for a pulse.
3. Rebecca **squeezed** the man's heart and **gave** him her breath.
4. She **kept** on doing so, even though it **didn't** really seem to work.
5. When Rebecca finally **stood up**, she was dizzy.

30 **1.** Missy was dictating conditions **which** were non-negotiable.
2. She wanted to work with a child **who** could be rescued from its fate.
3. Missy had a rule **which** was to leave after two years.
4. She liked children **who** didn't talk when they had nothing to say.
5. Romney had an accent **which** was typical of East London.

31 **1.** a guy – **bloke**
2. not long ago – **recently**
3. wearing glasses – **bespectacled**
4. perfectly – **impeccably**
5. to clean by using a cloth – **wipe**
6. be like – **resemble**
7. fascinated – **intrigued**

32 **1.** poor – **wealthy**
2. female – **male**
3. successor – **predecessor**
4. easy – **difficult**
5. gladly – **sadly**
6. irrelevant– **important**
7. successful – **doomed**

33 **1.** The magazines on the top shelf had cover girls who were showing their **buttocks**.
2. Romney hoped Otto's seed would **prove** to be wealthy.
3. A lot was written about Romney's affair in the **tabloids**.
4. Arthur **piled** the dirty dishes neatly.
5. For Missy, stoicism was a **virtue**.

34
- [X] He is not sure if he'll like the new baby.
  Er ist sich nicht sicher, ob er das neue Baby mögen wird.
- [ ] He doesn't look at the magazines with his mother's picture on the cover.
  Er schaut die Zeitschriften, auf deren Titelbild seine Mutter ist, nicht an.
- [X] Chocolate is one of his favourite sweets.
  Schokolade ist eine seiner Lieblingssüßigkeiten.
- [ ] He is quite naïve for an eight-year-old boy.
  Für einen achtjährigen Jungen ist er ziemlich naiv.
- [X] He is afraid of the myth about Artemis.
  Er hat Angst vor dem Artemis-Mythos.
- [X] He would have named his sister "Jane".
  Er hätte seiner Schwester den Namen "Jane" gegeben.
- [ ] He reads the article about his mum carefully.
  Den Artikel über seine Mutter las er gründlich.

35 **1.** The baby received **round-the-clock** attention.
2. The Primrose Hill household was running smoothly.
3. Arthur's parents have joint custody.
4. Romney wants to go on a detox meditation.
5. The band was on a world tour.
6. Arthur told Missy **matter-of-factly** that she had to stay with him.
7. Missy was looking forward to some **leaf-kicking** time.

36 **1.** There was no taxi at the airport **when** they arrived.
2. **If** there was a reservation for them, the receptionist should know.
3. **If** I can find a second-hand book, I won't buy a new one.
4. Why should I buy a new book **when** I know I can get the same one cheaper in an Oxfam shop?
5. **If** Missy didn't care for Arthur, then who would?
6. **If** this was to be the life of luxury they had dreamed of, then it was not very impressive.

37 **abandon – nonchalant – travel – leg – girl – libraries – sterling**

38 „Das ist Pech." – **„Bad luck."**
„Es sind schlechte Zeiten." – **„These are bad times."**
„Wie schade." – **„What a pity."**
„Hat jemand nach uns gefragt?" – **„Did anyone ask for us?"**

39 **1.** Missy and Arthur had **enough** money to continue their journey.
2. The banner declared its message in **large** capitals.
3. Lulu and Romney remained unreachable **by all means**.
4. Neither Arthur nor Missy were **much** in the mood for history and culture.
5. The "Wolpertinger" looked like a mix of several animals plus something **more** frightening.

40 **1.** [c] Where is the ticket sales desk? **Over there.**
2. [a] Who gave Arthur some cake? **The proprietress of the guesthouse did.**
3. [d] How long was Arthur sobbing? **For hours.**
4. [g] Why were Arthur's eyes red? **Because he had been crying.**
5. [e] When will Arthur leave Missy? **One day.**
6. [b] Who cried "shut up" several times? **Arthur did.**
7. [f] Who put Arthur to bed? **Missy did.**

41

1. nevertheless	**still**
2. in the near future	**soon**
3. winding	**snaking**
4. precious metal	**silver**
5. to cry	**shout**
6. summer shoes	**sandals**
7. a distinctive noise	**sound**

Wörterverzeichnis

A

A and E (= accident and emergency) Notaufnahme
abandon Unbekümmertheit
abandoned: to be (was/were – been) abandoned by aufgegeben werden von
to abdicate one's responsibility sich seiner Verantwortung entziehen
aberration Fehltritt
abortion Abtreibung
about: to be (was/were – been) about to im Begriff sein zu
abroad im Ausland
absence Fehlen von; Abwesenheit
abundant üppig
to abuse missbrauchen
abyss Abgrund
accompaniment: to the accompaniment of zur Begleitung von
accord: in accord with in Übereinstimmung mit
account Konto
to account for something für etwas verantwortlich sein
accustomed: to be (was/were – been) accustomed to doing something gewohnt sein, etwas zu tun
achievement Erfolg
acid LSD (= Droge)
acquaintance Bekanntenkreis
acquainted: to be (was/were – been) acquainted with someone mit jemandem Kontakt haben
to acquire erstehen; annehmen
across the board durch die Bank
additional zusätzlich
adenoids Rachenmandeln
adept: to be (was/were – been) adept at Experte sein in
admirer Verehrer(in)
adolescence Jugendzeit
adolescent jugendlich
to adorn verzieren
adult Erwachsener
to advance sich nähern
advertising material Werbematerial
advocate Rechtsanwalt
to afford sich leisten
agitated aufgewühlt; aufgeregt
agitatedly aufgeregt
ahead of vor
air Auftreten
alien fremdartig
to alight from aussteigen aus
to align with bündig ausrichten an
all over the place überall
allowance Zulage
aloft in die Höhe
altogether vollkommen
alumnus Absolvent

alumni Absolventen
to amaze erstaunen
amber bernsteinfarben
ambrosial köstlich
American flagfish Floridakärpfling
amongst inmitten
anchor Anker
ancient uralt
anew von Neuem
ankle Knöchel
announcement Anzeige
to annoy nerven
anonymous anonym
antenatal clinic Schwangerenberatung
anxiety Ängstlichkeit
apoplectic kurz vorm Schlaganfall
appalling entsetzlich
to approach something etwas angehen
apron Schürze
arguments Auseinandersetzungen
arse: my arse meine Scheiße
articulate redegewandt
Arts Geisteswissenschaften
as: it's as good as it gets besser wird's nicht mehr
ash Eschenholz
ashamed: to be (was/were – been) ashamed sich schämen
to ask for trouble Ärger heraufbeschwören
to assault überfallen
assembled versammelt
astonishing erstaunlich
to atone büßen
to attach anhängen, verbinden
attempt Versuch
attic Dachboden
avian world Vogelwelt
to avoid vermeiden
awfully furchtbar
awkward unangenehm
awkwardly linkisch
azure azurblau

B

back problems Rückenschmerzen
badly dringend
baked beans weiße Bohnen in Tomatensoße
to bang someone up jemanden einbuchten
banister Treppengeländer
to bankroll finanzieren
bar Riegel
bar chart Säulendiagramm
baronial feudal
bath Badewanne
battle Kampf
battlement Zinne
Bavarian bayerisch
bawling plärrend
bay Erker
to bay bellen
to be (was/were – been) with somebody (mental) dabei sein
to bear (bore – borne) out bestätigen
to bear: it doesn't bear thinking about man darf gar nicht darüber nachdenken
beard Bart
to beat (beat – beaten) to a pulp zu Brei schlagen
beat sergeant Streifenpolizist

to bed someone jemanden ins Bett bekommen
beforehand zuvor
belly Bauch
belly-up mit dem Bauch nach oben
bemused ratlos
to bend (bent – bent) double over someone/something sich tief über jemanden/etwas beugen
bent gebeugt
bespectacled eine Brille tragend
beyond belief unglaublich
beyond translation unübersetzbar
the Births and Deaths column Spalte mit Geburts- und Todesanzeigen
birth certificate Geburtsurkunde
birthright Geburtsrecht
bitch Miststück
to blame (someone) (jemandem) die Schuld geben
blank-faced ausdruckslos
blaze of glory in Glanz und Gloria
bleached ausgebleicht
bloater Fettqualle
bloke Typ
blood-cold kalt
blossom Blüte
blow Hieb
blur undeutliches Bild
to boak kotzen
to boil toben
boiled-egg tea aus gekochten Eiern bestehende Zwischenmahlzeit
bonehead Dummkopf
bonny hübsch
booming dröhnend
bossy herrisch
Botanics (= Botanical Gardens) botanischer Garten
to bother belästigen
to bother to sich die Mühe machen, zu
to bounce off abprallen
bouncy castle Hüpfburg
bound: to be (was/were – been) bound for unterwegs sein nach
bow Bogen
bowl Schale
bra BH
Braille Blindenschrift
brain haemorrhage Hirnblutung
brainwashing Gehirnwäsche
brainy gescheit
to brandish schwingen
breakneck halsbrecherisch
bridal magazine Brautzeitschrift
briskly forsch
to brood over something über etwas brüten
bubble Blase
bubbling blubbernd
to build (built – built) from aufbauen von
to bulge hervortreten
bullet Patronenkugel
to bully schikanieren
bully Tyrann
bump kleine Beule (früher Schwangerschaftsbauch)
to bump onto aufsetzen auf
burst Ausbruch
to burst (burst – burst) platzen
butterfly Schmetterling
buttocks Hintern

by all means absolut
to bypass umgehen
bystander Zuschauer

C

to cackle gackern
camomile tea Kamillentee
can Dose
cancer Krebs
canvas Leinwand
capable of fähig zu
capital Hauptstadt
capital letter Großbuchstabe
car boot sale (eine Art) Flohmarkt
cardboard tube Papprӧhre
carefree sorglos
carp Karpfen
carrier bags Tragetaschen
to carry a child ein Kind austragen
casserole Auflauf
to cast (cast – cast) one's mind back to something an etwas zurückdenken
casually beiläufig
casualty department Unfallstation
to catalogue katalogisieren
to catch (caught – caught) a bus einen Bus nehmen
to catch (caught – caught) someone's eye mit jemandem Blickkontakt herstellen
to caution warnen
caveat Vorbehalt
ceilidh schottischer Unterhaltungsabend
cereal Frühstücksflocken
chance: by chance zufällig
to channel auf etwas richten
charge: to be (was/were – been) in charge die Verantwortung tragen
charges: one's charges Kinder, die man betreut
chariot Triumphwagen
to chart erfassen
chase Jagd
cheek Wange
to cheer someone up jemanden aufmuntern
cheerfully fröhlich
chief inspector Hauptkommissar
to chill abkühlen
chips Pommes frites
chocolate buttons Schokolinsen
to choke on something an etwas ersticken; sich an etwas verschlucken
to chop hauen
to chortle glucksen
Christ! Herrgott!
Christ: for Christ's sake Herrgott noch mal
to christen taufen
chummy kumpelhaft
to claim something auf etwas Anspruch erheben
clarion hell klingend
clatter Scheppern
clifftop Klippenrand
to clink klirren
to clip someone's wings jemandem die Flügel stutzen
cloak Umhang
cloaked: to be (was/were – been) cloaked verhüllt sein
to clog up verstopfen

close up aus der Nähe
to clutch umklammern
to cock one's head den Kopf schief legen
cocoon Kokon
cod Kabeljau
coffin Sarg
to coil sich winden
collar Kragen
to come (came – come) across something auf etwas stoßen
to come clean beichten
comedian Komiker
compact Puderdose
to compose erdichten
to compress drücken
to conceive empfangen
concern Sorge
conclusion Schlussfolgerung
concrete Beton
to condemn verurteilen
to confide to someone jemandem etwas anvertrauen
conger eel Seeaal
congregated: to be (was/were – been) congregated versammelt sein
connecting flight Anschlussflug
conscience Gewissen
consensus Übereinkunft
to consider bedenken
conspiratorial verschwörerisch
contacts Kontaktlinsen
to contain beinhalten
to contaminate verunreinigen
contemplation Betrachtung
contentedly zufrieden
contest Wettbewerb
in contravention of verstoßen gegen
to contrive (to): he contrived to es gelang ihm
convivality Fröhlichkeit
coral Koralle
corner shop Tante-Emma-Laden
cot Kinderbett
cough sweets Hustenbonbons
to court umwerben
courtship Umwerben
to covet begehren
crab Krabbe
crack Ritze
to crack brechen; (Gelenke) knacken lassen
cramp Krampf
crap Scheiß-
crappy Scheiß-
to crease oneself sich vor Lachen kringeln
Crete Kreta
crime Verbrechen
crop Ernte
to cross one's heart and hope to die großes Ehrenwort geben
crown Krone
to crush to death erdrücken
crystalline kristallen
to cuddle umarmen
culprit Übeltäter
cunt Fotze
cunting Scheiß-
curdled geronnen
curious neugierig; seltsam
curiously seltsam
curlicue Schnörkel
curriculum Lehrplan

to curse fluchen
to cushion abfedern
cushiony kissenweich
cut-glass geschliffen
cutting Zeitungsausschnitt

D

to dab abtupfen
damply feucht
to dangle baumeln
Danish pastry Blätterteiggebäck
to dart umherschießen
dashed zerschlagen
to dawdle trödeln
Day Saver Tageskarte
debauched verkommen
to decapitate köpfen
decent anständig; nett
defiance Trotz
to deflate zusammensinken
degree (Hochschul-)Abschluss
deliberately absichtlich
delicacy Feingefühl
delicate zart
delicately vorsichtig
deluge (Regen-)Guss
denim smock Hängekleid aus Jeans
derogatory abfällig
despair Verzweiflung
to despise verachten
to detach oneself from sich lösen von
detached frei stehend
detox Entgiftungs-
dial Anzeige
to digest vorkauen (eigentl.: verdauen)
dire dringlich
disappointment Enttäuschung
disapprovingly missbilligend
disbelief Unglaube
discontentedly missmutig
disfigured entstellt
disgusting widerlich
dislocated ausgerenkt
dismissively ablehnend
display of Vorführung
to dispose of something etwas beseitigen
distracted abgelenkt
district nurse Gemeindeschwester
divine göttlich
divorce Scheidung
dizzy schwindlig
dog handler Hundeführer
dogs' home Tierheim
domestic abuse Gewalt in der Familie
doomed zum Scheitern verurteilt
dope Marihuana
dopey dämlich
dotted verstreut
double doppelt
double-glazing Doppelverglasung
downpour Platzregen
to drag ziehen; zerren
to draw (drew – drawn) up a shortlist eine Liste der engeren Auswahl anfertigen
drawbridge Zugbrücke
drawing room Salon
to dread fürchten
dreary trostlos
to drench eintauchen
drop Sinken

to drop einwerfen
to drop dead tot umfallen
drowning Ertrinken
dry-eyed ungerührt
dull-witted einfältig
Dux of the school Schulbester
dying: to be (was/were – been) dying to do something darauf brennen, etwas zu tun

E

eager for begierig auf
eardrum Trommelfell
to ease off entspannen
to eavesdrop lauschen
eccentricity Eigenartigkeit
edge Kante
effortlessly mühelos
elation Hochgefühl
to elbow one's way out sich hinausdrängeln
elocution Sprechtechnik
embarrassed verlegen
encased ummantelt
encounter Begegnung
enemy Feind
enigmatic hintergründig
to enjoy oneself sich amüsieren
enough: to be (was/were – been)… enough soweit ganz … sein
to enquire of sich erkundigen bei
enraged aufgebracht
en-suite mit eigenem Badezimmer
ENT consultant (= ear, nose and throat consultant) HNO-Arzt
to entangle verheddern
entirely völlig
entity Einheit
equally ebenso
to erupt ausbrechen
eternity Ewigkeit
eugh igitt
euphemism beschönigende Beschreibung
to evaporate verfliegen
eventually schließlich
to exasperate entnerven
except nur dass
to exhale ausatmen
exhibit Ausstellungsstück
expectant erwartungsvoll
expense: on someone else's expenses auf Kosten eines anderen
extinct ausgestorben

F

face Miene
fag Kippe
to fail nicht bestehen
fairground Jahrmarkt
fairly ziemlich
fairyland Märchenland
familiar: to be (was/were – been) on familiar terms with vertraut sein mit
fanciful abstrus
to fancy liebäugeln mit
to fart furzen
fashionable in Mode
fatal tödlich
fate Schicksal
fatherhood Vaterschaft
fault Schuld
faux- unecht
favour basket Geschenkkörbchen

feature Gesichtszug
to feature on the curriculum auf dem Lehrplan stehen
feeble lahm
feline katzenartig
fellow ebenbürtig
fertility Fruchtbarkeit
fibre Faser
fighter pilot Kampfpilot
file Aktenordner
to file zu den Akten legen
to file out nacheinander hinausgehen
to find (found – found) something hard to believe etwas kaum glauben können
first: in the first place von vornherein
first-aider Ersthelfer(in)
first offence Straftat eines Ersttäters
fish tank Aquarium
fissure Spalt
fit: in a fit of in einem Anfall von
fitted wardrobe Einbauschrank
flap Schlag
to flash funkeln
flaw Fehler
flightless flugunfähig
flint Feuerstein
flock of sheep Schafherde
floundering zappelnd
to fly (flew – flown) into fliegen in
to flush erröten
to flutter sich unruhig bewegen
foil Folie
football pitch Fußballplatz
forced: to be (was/were – been) forced to gezwungen sein zu
forearm Unterarm
forehead Stirn
foretelling Voraussage
forlorn verlassen
to fortify bestärken
to fracture zerteilen
fractured skull Schädelbruch
fragrance Duft
frantic wild
to freeze (froze – frozen) gefrieren
French knitting Stricken mit Strickliesel
French window Verandatür
fretful besorgt
frilled gerüscht
frond Wedel
froth Gischt
frown Stirnrunzeln
frumpy ohne Schick
fuelled angeheizt von
full of oneself eingebildet
full-length in voller Länge
funeral Begräbnisfeier
funeral pyre Scheiterhaufen
funeral service Trauergottesdienst
funereal gedrückt, trübsinnig
fungal growth Pilzbefall
further weitere
fuzzy undeutlich

G

gaily fröhlich
game of catch Fangen
to gargle gurgeln
garment rail Kleiderstange
gasp hörbares Einatmen
to gather zusammenkommen

gay schwul
to gaze at betrachten
gear Ausrüstung
geek Streber
gently sanft
gesture Geste
to get (got – got/gotten) a shot at (doing) something sich an einer Sache versuchen
to get away with something mit etwas davonkommen
to get stuck festsitzen
to get thumped geschlagen werden
gift Geschenk
gills Kiemen
to give (gave – given) in to nachgeben
to give (gave – given) someone the creeps jemandem nicht geheuer sein
glacial eisig
glaikit (schottisch für) dumm
to glare starren
gloom Düsterheit
glowering vor Wut kochend
to go (went – gone) into labour Wehen bekommen
to go out of one's way sich große Mühe geben
gorgeously wunderschön
gormless dämlich
to gossip tratschen
grateful dankbar
grating krächzend
grave Grab
gravelly heiser
gravy Soße
grief-stricken kummervoll
grimly eisern
grip Griff
to groan knurren
grommet Paukenröhrchen
gross abstoßend
grounded: to be (was/were – been) grounded Hausarrest haben
grown-up Erwachsener
grubby dreckig
to grunt grunzen
guilty schuldbewusst
to gulp hinunterkippen
to gush sprudeln

H

to hack off abhacken
haddock Schellfisch
hairline fracture Fissur
half-term Schulferien (nach ca. der Hälfte eines Trimesters)
hall of residence Studentenwohnheim
hallway Flur
handkerchief Taschentuch
handsome gut aussehend
haphazard planlos
to harness vorspannen
harsh barsch
haste: in haste in Eile
hatred of starke Abneigung gegen
haul Beute; Fang
to haul schleppen
to have (had – had) a heroic ring to it heldenhaft klingen
to have it off with someone es mit jemandem treiben
to have no idea keine Ahnung haben

to have none of it (von etwas) nichts wissen wollen
hawk-headed mit einem Falkenkopf
hazard Gefahr
headlong kopfüber
headphones Kopfhörer
headstone Grabstein
hero Held
hey presto Simsalabim; sofort
hiccup Schluckauf
hideously schrecklich
high: to be (was/were – been) high as a kite total high sein
High Court oberstes Gericht
Highers schottische Hochschulreife
Highlands schottisches Hochland
highly strung überspannt
high-spirited übermütig
hindsight: with hindsight rückblickend
history lecturer Geschichtsdozent
to hit (hit – hit) someone like jemanden treffen wie
holiday: on holiday im Urlaub
honeymoon Flitterwochen
hook Haken
hound Jagdhund
to howl with laughter in brüllendes Gelächter ausbrechen
huge riesig
to hurry sich beeilen
hushed leise

I

ice-lolly Eis am Stiel
ICU (= intensive care unit) Intensivstation
idly in aller Ruhe
ill krank
ill at ease unbehaglich
illegitimate unehelich
illicit verboten
imaginary gedacht
immortal unsterblich
impeccably makellos
impenetrable unergründlich
imposing imponierend
improvement Verbesserung
to incant aufsagen
incidental nebensächlich
incinerated: to be (was/were – been) incinerated eingeäschert werden
incomprehensible unverständlich
to increase vergrößern
indifferent mittelmäßig
indignantly entrüstet
industriously eifrig
infinitely unendlich
infuriatingly zum Verzweifeln
to inherit erben
innards Innereien
innocent unbeteiligt
insomniac Person, die an Schlaflosigkeit leidet
instead stattdessen
to instill beibringen
intent: to be (was/were – been) intent on doing something fest entschlossen sein, etwas zu tun
to interfere sich einmischen
to intimidate einschüchtern
intrigued by fasziniert von
intrusion Einmischung
invariably ausnahmslos

invisibility Unsichtbarkeit
invisible unsichtbar
involuntary unwillkürlich
irresistible unwiderstehlich
itinerary Reiseablauf

J

jaw Kiefer
jeelie (= jelly) Marmelade
to jilt someone jemandem den Laufpass geben
to join sich anschließen
joint custody gemeinsames Sorgerecht
jumble sale Flohmarkt
junk Schrott

K

keen: to be (was/were – been) keen on something auf etwas scharf sein
to keep (kept – kept) mum about schweigen über
to keep one step ahead einen Schritt voraus sein
to keep one's own counsel seine Meinung für sich behalten
kelp Seetang
kettle Teekessel
kin verwandt
kind nett
kirk (schott. für) Kirche
kitchen roll Küchenpapierrolle
to kneel (knelt – knelt) down niederknien
to knock someone off balance jemanden aus dem Gleichgewicht bringen
knocked: to be (was/were – been) knocked unconscious bewusstlos geschlagen werden
to knot verknoten
knowledgeable wissend
Kraut abwertende Bezeichnung für einen Deutschen

L

to lack: he lacks something es fehlt ihm an etwas
lacking: to be (was/were – been) lacking in es fehlen lassen an
to lag behind zurückbleiben
lager Lagerbier
lap dog Schoßhund
lardy fettig
latter: the latter Letzteres
to lay (laid – laid) a bet that wetten, dass
to leaf through durchblättern
leaking undicht
least sporty unsportlichste
left: to be (was/were – been) left stranded seinem Schicksal überlassen werden
leg Etappe
to let (let – let) go of the reins die Zügel loslassen
to lick lecken
for life lebenslänglich
lifetime lebenslänglich
to lift klauen
likely wahrscheinlich
lilac Flieder
to limp on sich dahinschleppen
listlessly teilnahmslos
litter Wurf

loaf Brotlaib
to loiter herumlungern
to look at something this way etwas mal so sehen
to loom above someone jemanden überragen
love-rat untreuer Mann
ludicrously aberwitzig
lump Geschwulst
lunatic irre
to lure anlocken
to lurk lauern

M

maître d' Oberkellner
major wesentlich
to make (made – made) a point of Wert legen auf
to make an effort sich Mühe geben
to make do with sich begnügen mit
to make one's bed sein Bett machen
to make up wiedergutmachen
malevolence Böswilligkeit
malt Malz
mammal Säugetier
maniacally wie verrückt
manners Umgangsformen
to mar verunstalten
marble Marmor
to mark korrigieren
mashed potatoes Kartoffelbrei
master bedroom großes Schlafzimmer
to materialize auftauchen
maternal mütterlich
maternal grandmother Großmutter mütterlicherseits
maternity nurse Säuglingsschwester
matter-of-factly sachlich
to meander umherschlendern
a mechanic's hand ein Händchen für Motoren
Mediterranean Mittelmeer
meek sanftmütig
mere mortals Normalsterbliche
mermaid Meerjungfrau
mess Durcheinander
messy unordentlich
metabolic disease Stoffwechselkrankheit
metempsychosis Seelenwanderung
midwife Hebamme
to mill around herumlaufen
mince Hackfleisch
to mind: she doesn't mind es ist ihr egal
to mingle sich vermischen
minister Pfarrer
to minister to sich kümmern um
minor unbedeutend
misery Misere
to moan stöhnen
moat Burggraben
mobile (phone) Handy
mock-Tudor pseudo-Tudor
moderation: in moderation in Maßen
modest bescheiden
months: to be (was/were – been) five months gone im sechsten Monat schwanger sein
mood Laune; Stimmung
more than mehr als
moron Schwachkopf

mother-of-pearl Perlmutt
mourner Trauernde(r)
to muffle dämpfen
mumsy matronenhaft
murmur of agreement einvernehmliches Gemurmel
mushroom Pilz
muted gedämpft
to mutter brummeln

N

to nag herumnörgeln
to name but um nur … zu nennen
nanny Kindermädchen
napkin Serviette
navy Marine
neat hübsch; ordentlich
necessity Notwendigkeit
neck bones Halswirbel
neck collar Halskrause
to need a hand Hilfe brauchen
need: to be (was/were – been) in need of brauchen
neither keiner
neither: to be neither here nor there keine Rolle spielen
nereid Nereid (Meeresnymphen in der griech. Mythologie)
never-made nie gemacht
new-mown frisch gemäht
newsagents Zeitungsladen
nonchalant gleichgültig
non-negotiable nicht verhandelbar
norks Titten
nun Nonne

O

obediently gehorsam
obeisance Ehrerbietung
obituary Nachruf
obscenity Obszönität
obsessed besessen
obsessive besessen
occasional gelegentlich
to occupy beschäftigen
to occur geschehen
odd seltsam
often as not meistens
olden: in the olden days früher
old-fashioned altmodisch
on a large scale im großen Maßstab
on one's own allein
one: the one and only der, die, das Einzige
one way or another irgendwie
oppressive beklemmend
to opt for sich entscheiden für
opulence Üppigkeit
ordinariness Gewöhnlichkeit
orphan Waisen-
orphanage Waisenhaus
outcome Ergebnis
out-of-the-blue aus heiterem Himmel
outsider Außenseiter
overenthusiastic überfreundlich
overexposed zur Schau gestellt
to overload überladen
overweight übergewichtig
overwhelming überwältigend
to own up zugeben

P

pal Kumpel
pale-and-prone-to-dermatitis blass und zu entzündlichen Reaktionen neigend
a pan of milk Milchtopf
parachutist Fallschirmspringer
paramedic Sanitäter
parents' evening Elternabend
to partake (partook – partaken) of teilhaben an
particular Merkmal
to paste (auf-)kleben
paternity Vaterschaft
pathetic erbärmlich
patio Terrasse
paunchy dickbäuchig
to paw scharren
peach Pfirsich
peculiarly eigenartig
to peel off abziehen von
pepper grinder Pfeffermühle
to perch against an ... drücken
perfunctory oberflächlich
to perk up die Ohren spitzen
to persecute verfolgen
pet Haustier
petal Blütenblatt
philanderer Schürzenjäger
phrase Redensart
to pick one's nose in der Nase bohren
pictorial illustriert
piglet Ferkel
to pile aufeinanderstapeln
pillar Säule
to pinch zwicken
pinched verkniffen
pipe Pfeife
plague pustules Pestbeulen
to plait flechten
planked verschalt
to plaster (an-)klatschen
plastic surgery Schönheitschirurgie
playground Pausenhof
playlet Schauspiel; Stück
pleasant nett; angenehm
to plod trotten
plump rundlich
to poke into die Nase in ... stecken
poke Tüte
politely höflich
to pool sich sammeln
to pore over something über etwas brüten
pork Schweinefleisch
porn mags Pornohefte
portcullis Fallgatter
pose Haltung
possession: to be (was/were – been) in possession of im Besitz sein von
possibly wohl
pot-luck supper Abendessen, zu dem jeder Gast eine Speise mitbringt
pouchy sackartig (hängend)
to pounce einen Satz machen
poured gegossen
to power mit Strom versorgen
powerlessness Machtlosigkeit
precariously gefährlich
precious kostbar
predecessor Vorgänger(in)

prefix Vorsilbe
pre-literate vor der Entwicklung einer geschriebenen Sprache
premature frühzeitig
pre-prandial vor dem Essen
pre-sixteenth century vor dem 16. Jahrhundert entstanden
to presoak vorab einweichen
to pretend so tun, als ob
previous vorangegangen
prey: to be (was/were – been) prey to something von etwas befallen werden
prick Schwanz
primary-school Grundschul-
primer Fibel
primeval urzeitlich
print: in print abgedruckt
pristine makellos
professed bekennend
profound tiefsinnig
property Grundstück
to propose to somebody jemandem einen Heiratsantrag machen
proprietress Besitzerin
prospect Aussicht
prostitute Prostituierte
protectively beschützend
to prove sich erweisen
to provide zur Verfügung stellen
psychotropic drug Psychopharmakon
publicist Pressesprecher(in)
to pull through durchkommen
punch Boxhieb
punchline Pointe
punishment Strafe
puppy Welpe
to purr schnurren
purposefulness Entschlossenheit
pus Eiter
push-and-pull lawnmower Handrasenmäher
puzzled verwundert

Q

queue Warteschlange
queue jumping Vordrängeln
to quiver zittern

R

to race against um die Wette laufen mit
rack Regal
to raise one's voice die Stimme erheben
rank Reihe; Stand
rank ranzig
to rant schimpfen
rapist Vergewaltiger
raptorial räuberisch
realm (König-)Reich
reasonable vernunftbetont
reassurance Beruhigung
to rebuke tadeln
recently kürzlich
reckless unbekümmert
to reckon glauben
to recognize wiedererkennen
record Eintrag ins Strafregister; Beleg
recorder Blockflöte
to rectify korrigieren
to redeem oneself from sich freimachen von

reed Schilf
to refer to bezeichnen als
refinement Vornehmheit
to refrain from doing something etwas unterlassen
refugee Flüchtling
regal majestätisch
relative Verwandter
to release freilassen
relief Erleichterung
relieved erleichtert
relish Genuss
reluctance Widerwillen
reluctant widerwillig
to remain bleiben
to remonstrate protestieren
to rend (rent – rent) zerreißen
to renege nicht Wort halten
to replenish wiederaufstocken
reputation Ruf
rescue Rettung
rescued: to be (was/were – been) rescued from bewahrt werden vor
to resemble someone jemandem ähnlich sehen
to resist widerstehen
resort Ausweg
responsibility Verantwortung
retsina geharzter griechischer Weißwein
to reveal preisgeben
to revive wiederbeleben
revolving abwechselnd
ribbon (Haar-)Band
ridden: to be (was/were – been) ridden with allergies von Allergien geplagt sein
ride Fahrgeschäft
ridiculous absurd
right gleich
ring-fenced an einen bestimmten Verwendungszweck gebunden
to rip someone off jemanden ausnehmen
risk assessor Risikoprüfer
to roast braten
rodent Nager
roll Brötchen
Roman römisch
rota (Dienst-)Plan
rousing mitreißend
royal Mitglied der königlichen Familie
rude unverschämt
rug Decke
rumble Donnern
to ruminate grübeln
rumour has it das Gerücht geht um
to run (ran – run) to doing something ausreichen, um etwas zu tun
run-of-the-mill alltäglich
ruse Trick
rush Binse
to rush rasen

S

sacrifice Opfer(gabe)
saggy ausgeleiert
sake: for the sake of um … willen
sales clerk Schalterangestellte
sales desk Ticketschalter
salmon Lachs
SAS (= Special Air Service) Spezialeinheit der britischen Armee

sated: to be (was/were – been) sated with gesättigt sein mit
satisfaction Genugtuung
saucer Untertasse
scale Schuppe
scary furchterregend
to scatter streuen
to scatter all over verstreuen über
scent Geruch
schemie school Schule voller Schüler aus ärmlichen Verhältnissen
school of dolphins Delfinschwarm
science block naturwissenschaftlicher Trakt
to scoop up aufheben
to scramble klettern
to scrape with beschmieren mit
to scrawl kritzeln
screwdriver Schraubenzieher
scuffed abgewetzt
scummy schmierig
to scurry out nach draußen huschen
sea bass Wolfsbarsch
seabed Meeresgrund
sealskin Seehundsfell
seating plan Sitzordnung
secondary school weiterführende Schule
to seem den Anschein haben
segs on shoes Schuhbeschläge
self-penned selbst verfasst
selfsufficient selbstständig
semi-detached villa Doppelhaushälfte
sense of belonging Zugehörigkeitsgefühl
sergeant Wachtmeister
to serve someone right jemandem recht geschehen
to settle on sich entscheiden für
several mehrere
to shag bumsen
shame schade
shared geteilt
shawl Tuch
sheer bloß
sheet Laken
shelf Regal
shell Muschel
shirtwaister Hemdblusenkleid
shite Scheiße
to shiver frösteln
shoal Schwarm
shoplifting Ladendiebstahl
shower of gold Goldregen
to shrink (shrank – shrunk) back zurückweichen
shrivelled verschrumpelt
to shrug mit den Schultern zucken
to shrug off abtun
to shuffle wälzen; hin und her schlurfen
to shush Pst! sagen
sibling(s) Geschwister
sick krank
silly albern
single-bedded room Einzelzimmer
to sip nippen
siren call Sirenengeheul
sitcom Sitcom (= Situationskomödie)
sixpence Sixpencestück
skate Rochen
skid-marked mit „Bremsspuren“

to skim-read (skim-read – skim-read) überfliegen
skin Haut
to skip überspringen
skip Müllcontainer
slab Platte
slack schlaff
to slam zuknallen
slashed durchgestrichen
to sleep (slept – slept) as soundly as fest schlafen wie
slice Scheibe
slightly leicht
to slump zusammensacken
smashed-up demoliert
to smirk grinsen
smooth glatt
smorgasbord of bunte Mischung von
smug selbstgefällig
to smuggle schmuggeln
to snake sich schlängeln
to snap reißen; schnauzen
to snap shut zuschnappen (lassen)
snappy starr
to sneeze niesen
to snicker kichern
to snigger kichern
to snore schnarchen
to snort with prusten vor
snotty verrotzt
to snuffle schniefen; schnaufen
soap opera Seifenoper
soiled verschmutzt
solemn ernst
solemnity: with solemnity mit großem Ernst
solid beständig
solitary einsam
soon-to-be zukünftig
soothing beruhigend
sorcerer Zauberer
sorely äußerst
sorrowful sorgenvoll
sorry jämmerlich
soubriquet Spitzname
source of paternity Abstammung
sow Sau
spasm Krampf
speccy four-eyes Brillenschlange
spectacles (= a pair of spectacles) Brille
speed dial Kurzwahl
speeding ticket Strafzettel für Geschwindigkeitsüberschreitung
spell Zauber
to spit (spat – spat) on spucken auf
spiteful gehässig
to splash platschen
to split (split – split) open aufschneiden
spoilt: to be (was/were – been) spoilt verdorben sein
to sport something etwas zur Schau tragen
to spot entdecken
spot Pickel
to sprawl ausstrecken
to sprinkle with bestreuen mit
to squash drücken
to squeeze pressen
squid Tintenfisch
to squint blinzeln
squirt Würstchen
stag Hirsch
to stagger taumeln

stained voller Flecken
stall (Messe-)Stand
stalwart getreuer Anhänger
to stand (stood – stood) for something etwas hinnehmen
to stand little chance of wenig Aussicht haben auf
to stand up straight gerade stehen
starch Stärke
to stare goggle-eyed so starren, dass einem fast die Augen aus dem Kopf fallen
state: in a state of disrepair in einem schlechten Zustand
steamy heiß
steel tips Stahlspitzen
steering wheel Lenkrad
step Takt
sterling Pfund (brit. Währung)
stern ernst
stick Stiel
to stick (stick – stuck) up herausragen
stiff steif
still trotzdem
stockinged: in stockinged feet in Strümpfen
stocky stämmig
stone-chip Ziersplitt
straight away sofort
to straighten glätten
strained angespannt
streak of lightning Blitz
to stride (strode – strode) across über … schreiten
to strike (struck – struck) someone jemandem in den Sinn kommen; jemanden mit einem Schlag klar werden
to strike aufschlagen auf
string Strähne; Gruppe
to stroke streicheln
stroll Spaziergang
strong gut
struck: to be (was/were – been) struck by lightning vom Blitz getroffen werden
stuck: to get (got – gotten) stuck stecken bleiben
stuff Zeug
to subdivide unterteilen
subject Unterrichtsfach
sublime erhaben
submission Unterwerfung
to submit to sich unterordnen
suburb Stadtrand
to suggest vermuten lassen
suggestible beeinflussbar
to suit somebody down to the ground für jemanden ideal sein
to sully besudeln
to suppose something etwas annehmen
supposed: to be (was/were – been) supposed to do something etwas tun sollen
suppressed unterdrückt
surface Oberfläche
surgeon Chirurg
suspension cable Aufhängungsseil
to swagger around herumstolzieren
to sweep (swept – swept) away davonspülen
swiftly eilig
sympathetic mitfühlend

T

tabloid (aus der) Boulevardpresse
tadpole Kaulquappe
to take (took – taken) after someone nach jemandem geraten
to take notice of someone jemandem Beachtung schenken
to take the biscuit den Vogel abschießen
takeaway Essen zum Mitnehmen
tally Strichliste
tannoy Lautsprecher
tantalizing verlockend
tap Wasserhahn
tarmac Asphalt
tea leichte Mahlzeit am Nachmittag
to tear (tore – torn) up zerreißen
tear-stained tränenüberströmt
teetotaller Antialkoholiker
tenement (house) Mietshaus
tepee Tipi
term Ausdruck
to terminate beenden
terrier-cross Terriermischling
terrified: to be (was/were – been) terrified of something große Angst vor etwas haben
tetchy reizbar
textile rooms Wandteppichsammlung
thank goodness Gott sei Dank
thinning dünner werdend
thread Klang
threat of rain Regengefahr
threshold Türschwelle
to thrive gedeihen
to thud dumpf schlagen
to thud off abprallen
thump dumpfer Schlag
thunder Donner
thunderbolt Donnerschlag
thunderclap Donnerschlag
to thwack schlagen
to tickle kitzeln
tidal wie eine Welle (wörtl.: Gezeiten-)
tight scharf
to tilt neigen
tinny blechern
to tip Trinkgeld geben
to tire müde werden
tom-tom Tamtam
tonsil Rachenmandel
toolbox Werkzeugkasten
top-heavy with voller
to toss zurückwerfen
touchingly rührend
tournament Wettkampf
to tower over someone/something über jemanden/etwas emporragen
traffic jam Verkehrsstau
traffic policeman Verkehrspolizist
trainer Turnschuh
to treat someone like jemanden wie … behandeln
to tremble zittern
tremor Zittern
tribeswoman Stammesfrau
to trip stolpern
to trot along nebenhertraben
trouble Mühe
troubleshooter Schlichter
to trust vertrauen

tube Schlauch
the tube (Londoner) U-Bahn
to tuck zurückstreifen
to tuck away verstauen
tumbler Trinkglas
to turn into something sich in etwas verwandeln
twice as much doppelt so viel

U

ugly hässlich
ultrasound photograph Ultraschallbild
unbearably unerträglich
unchecked unkontrolliert
to undo (undid – undone) öffnen
unearthly überirdisch
unfledged unreif
to unleash rauslassen, entfesseln
unlooked-for ungewollt
unnameable unsagbar
unnerved aus der Fassung
unruly widerspenstig
untroubling nicht störend
unwaveringly unerschütterlich
upper cut Aufwärtshaken
urge Drang
use Verwendung
useless piece of string Nichtsnutz
usher Platzanweiser

V

VA (= victim of accident) Unfallopfer
to vaccinate impfen
vaguely vage
Valentine Valentinsgruß
van Lieferwagen
varnished lackiert
veined adrig
velvet Samt
veneer Furnier
venue Veranstaltungsort
vertebra Wirbel (Plural: vertebrae)
vicious bösartig
victory Sieg
violence Gewalttätigkeit
virtue Tugend
vol-au-vent Pastete
volute Volute
to vomit erbrechen
vortex Strudel
vulnerable verletzlich

W

waistline Taille
waiting staff Servierpersonal
to wank wichsen
warily misstrauisch
warrior Krieger
waste Verschwendung
water nymph Wassernymphe
wealthy reich
wean Baby
weapon Waffe
weary erschöpft
to wed sich vermählen
wedding fair Hochzeitsmesse
wee klein
week: in weeks seit Wochen
weird komisch
well beyond: knowledgeable well beyond his years viel zu wissend für sein Alter
whatsoever überhaupt
to wheeze keuchen

whine Winseln
to whisk verquirlen
to whisk away entführen
whisky-sodden Whisky-trunken
whore Hure
whoremaister Hurenbock
whorl Windung
to will something to happen etwas durch Willenskraft geschehen lassen
willpower Willenskraft
window shopping Schaufensterbummel
to wink at someone jemandem zuzwinkern
to wipe abwischen
with zu
within innerhalb von
wolfkin Jungwolf
to wonder sich fragen
to work something out zu einem Schluss kommen
worn out verbraucht
worry Sorge
worse Schlimmeres
wretched erbärmlich
wrought-iron schmiedeeisern

Y

to yank zerren
yawn Gähnen
to yearn for something nach etwas verlangen
years: one's years sein Alter
to yell one's head off wie verrückt schreien
to yelp kreischen
yuck igitt